THE INTERPRETATION
OF VISUAL MOTION

The MIT Press Series in Artificial Intelligence

Artificial Intelligence: An MIT Perspective, Volume I: Expert Problem Solving, Natural Language Understanding, Intelligent Computer Coaches, Representation and Learning edited by Patrick Henry Winston and Richard Henry Brown, 1979

Artificial Intelligence: An MIT Perspective, Volume II: Understanding Vision, Manipulation, Computer Design, Symbol Manipulation edited by Patrick Henry Winston and Richard Henry Brown, 1979

NETL: A System for Representing and Using Real-World Knowledge by Scott Fahlman, 1979

The Interpretation of Visual Motion by Shimon Ullman, 1979

THE INTERPRETATION
OF VISUAL MOTION

Shimon Ullman

The MIT Press
Cambridge, Massachusetts, and London, England

PUBLISHER'S NOTE

This format is intended to reduce the cost of publishing certain works in book form and to shorten the gap between editorial preparation and final publication. The time and expense of detailed editing and composition in print have been avoided by photographing the text of this book directly from the author's computer printout.

Library of Congress Cataloging in Publication Data

Ullman, Shimon.
  The interpretation of visual motion.

  Bibliography: p.
  Includes index.
  1. Visual perception--Data processing. 2. Motion perception (Vision)--Data processing. I. Title.
BF241.U43   152.1'425   78-21092
ISBN 0-262-21007-X

To the memory of my father

DAVID THEODOR ULLMANN, M.D.

CONTENTS

SERIES FOREWORD

Artificial intelligence is the study of intelligence using the ideas and methods of computation. Unfortunately, a definition of intelligence seems impossible at the moment because intelligence appears to be an amalgam of so many information-processing and information-representation abilities.

Of course psychology, philosophy, linguistics, and related disciplines offer various perspectives and methodologies for studying intelligence. For the most part, however, the theories proposed in these fields are too incomplete and too vaguely stated to be realized in computational terms. Something more is needed, even though valuable ideas, relationships, and constraints can be gleaned from traditional studies of what are, after all, impressive existence proofs that intelligence is in fact possible.

Artificial intelligence offers a new perspective and a new methodology. Its central goal is to make computers intelligent, both to make them more useful and to understand the principles that make intelligence possible. That intelligent computers will be extremely useful is obvious. The more profound point is that artificial intelligence aims to understand intelligence using the ideas and methods of computation, thus offering a radically new and different basis for theory formation. Most of the people doing artificial intelligence believe that these theories will apply to any intelligent information processor, whether biological or solid state.

There are side effects that deserve attention, too. Any program that will successfully model even a small part of intelligence will be inherently massive and complex. Consequently, artificial intelligence continually confronts the limits of computer science technology. The problems encountered have been hard enough and interesting enough to seduce artificial intelligence people into working on them with enthusiasm. It is natural, then, that there has been a steady flow of ideas from artificial intelligence to computer science, and the flow shows no sign of abating.

The purpose of this MIT Press Series in Artificial Intelligence is to provide people in many areas, both professionals and students, with timely, detailed information about what is happening on the frontiers in research centers all over the world.

Patrick Henry Winston
Mike Brady

PREFACE

The study described in this manuscript reflects an evolution of approaches towards the study of visual perception. When I first became intrigued by the phenomena of visual perception, I hoped to approach them through the study of the anatomy and physiology of the visual system. For reasons which will be mentioned in the introduction, it became increasingly clear that a more abstract study of the computations performed in the course of visual analysis might help to supplement, and sometimes guide, the study of the visual system. The "do it yourself" methodology employed in the field of Artificial Intelligence seemed to offer potential advantages. The underlying motivation was to use the construction of workable schemes, that can actually perform certain tasks which are performed by the visual system, as vehicles for investigating the problems faced by the system and its methods for solving them.

When I came to the Artificial Intelligence Laboratory of the Massachusetts Institute of Technology, I was fortunate to meet D. Marr who, during that period, laid the foundations for the computational study of Vision. I am deeply indebted to him for his invaluable help ever since, and for close and stimulating interactions. The computational study of Vision at M.I.T. gradually gave rise to an informal, but highly interactive group, both at M.I.T. and elsewhere. I have benefited from interactions with many "members" of this group: T. Poggio of the Max-Plank Institut fur Biologische Kybernetik at Tubingen, W. Richards of the M.I.T. Psychology department, K. Stevens, E. Grimson and E. Hildreth of the M.I.T. A.I. Laboratory who made many valuable comments on drafts of this manuscript, K. Nishihara, and others. This work would not have been possible without the unique environment and facilities available at the Artificial Intelligence Laboratory.

I thank the Institute for Advanced Computation at Sunnyvale, California, for their invitation and support during the summer of 1977, the Proceedings of the Royal Society for permission to reproduce parts of [Ullman, 1978b] including Figures 1 and 2 there, and Karen Prendergast for preparing the drawings.

Finally, I wish to express my gratitude to my wife, Chana, for her encouragement and support.

This report describes research done at the Artificial Intelligence Laboratory of the Massachusetts Institute of Technology. Support for the laboratory's artificial intelligence research is provided in part by the Advanced Research Project Agency of the Department of Defence under Office of Naval Research contract N00014-75-C-0643. The work was also supported by NSF grant 77-07569-MCS.

THE INTERPRETATION
OF VISUAL MOTION

THE INTERPRETATION OF VISUAL MOTION

INTRODUCTION

1. Theoretical Preliminaries

The interpretation of visual motion is the process by which a description of the environment in terms of objects, their three-dimensional shape, and their motion through space is constructed on the basis of the changing image that reaches the eye.

The study described in this manuscript is aimed towards a computational theory of this process. It thus has a twofold goal. First, to investigate the process of interpreting visual motion. Second, to illustrate the computational approach to the study of visual perception. Some of the general issues underlying the computational approach are briefly discussed in this introduction. Others are deferred to later chapters (primarily Chapters 3 and 4), where they are accompanied by examples from the theory of visual motion.

Underlying the computational theory of visual perception is the notion that the human visual system can be viewed as a symbol-manipulating system [Marr, 1976]. The computation it supports is, at least in part, *the construction of useful descriptions of the visible environment.* An immediate consequence of this view is the distinction that can be drawn between the physical embodiment of the symbols manipulated by the system on the one hand, and the meaning of these symbols on the other. One can study, in other words, the *computation* performed by the system almost independently of the physical *mechanisms* supporting the computation.

It seems that before the notion of computing machines came into existence, the role that a physical device might play in the processing of information was somewhat difficult to grasp. One corollary of this difficulty was the concentration on the study of the physical structure of the brain as the means for appreciating its functions. Following the development of computers and computation theory, it became clear that a distinction can be drawn between the study of a process in the abstract, and the study of the physical structure embodying this process. The physical system and the computation it supports are, of course, related, but should not be equated. One reason for the distinction between mechanism and computation is that not all of the physical events in a symbol-manipulating system are meaningful at the computational level. Let me illustrate this point by an example from a simple computing device, the electronic calculator. Some of the events in the electronic calculator have their meaning in the domain of arithmetic. Other events and components, e.g. those inside the power supply, do not have such a meaning. The theory of the electronic calculator and the theory of the computation it performs are consequently distinct and non-isomorphic. But the distinction between mechanism and computation runs deeper than this non-isomorphism: the logic governing the computation is not entirely expressible in terms of the physical system. For example, the fact that a standard pocket calculator presents only the first eight digits of the square root of the number 2.0 is a property of the particular device in question. The fact that this number cannot be represented by *any* finite decimal belongs to a different realm, i.e. to the theory of arithmetic. Furthermore, the theory of the mechanism and the theory of the computation deal with different entities. The theory of the calculator deals with electronic circuits, currents, and voltages. The theory of what is being computed, on the other hand, deals with arithmetic objects.

To summarize the above discussion: whenever we say that a certain device can be viewed as a symbolic system, we imply that some of the events within the system can be consistently interpreted as having a meaning in a certain domain. One can thus investigate the physical device, or study what is being computed. The two studies are not identical, and neither is completely reducible to the other.

The implication of the foregoing discussion for the study of the visual system is that this study should include at least two interrelated but distinct parts: the study of the computation, and the study of the mechanisms that support it. The computational investigation concerns the nature of the internal representations used by the visual system and the processes by which they are derived. The study of the mechanisms concerns, in the case of biological visual systems, the neural circuitry in which they are implemented [Marr & Poggio, 1977].

The discussed dichotomy between mechanism and computation raises the following problem: How is one to discover the computations performed by the visual system? One possible approach is to use anatomical and physiological studies of the physical system as leads for unraveling the computations it performs. Another approach, common in psychological investigations, is to study the observable behavior of the system in terms of certain input-output relationships. In this work emphasis is placed on a third approach: studies of the tasks accomplished by the visual system in order to investigate the computations it performs. Such a study begins by defining the goal of the visual task at hand. In the exact formulation of the goal, psychophysical data may be of key value. For instance, following Julesz' studies of stereo vision [Julesz, 1971], one computational goal can be formulated as the extraction of a disparity map from a pair of images without using monocular clues. Once the goal has been formulated, the problems involved in achieving this goal can be addressed. The objective of this endeavor is to formulate a theory that will account for the input-output relationships of the system under idealized conditions [1]. In formulating the computational theory, a major portion concerns the discovery of the implicit assumptions utilized by the visual system. Briefly, these are valid assumptions about the environment that are incorporated into the computation. They will be further elaborated in Chapter 4, where the notion of "reflective constraints" is discussed.

The computational theory can be followed by a study of the particular algorithm used by the visual system in achieving the task in question. A secondary motivation behind the construction of an algorithm is that it helps one to appreciate problems that otherwise tend to pass unnoticed. The difference between a computational theory and a particular algorithm that implements it is somewhat analogous to the distinction between a mathematical function and a procedure used by a computer. The former is more general and specifies the overall input-output relationships, while the latter specifies a particular implementation using a given set of primitive operations (see [Marr 1977a] for a discussion of "methods" and "algorithms"). Psychophysical data might again be of help, in constraining the range of algorithms to be considered. Additional constraints are imposed by the requirement that the algorithm be biologically feasible, as discussed in Chapter 3.

The problem of interpreting visual motion is approached in this work by dividing it into two parts: the *correspondence* problem and the *3-D interpretation* problem. The correpondence problem is that of identifying a portion of the changing visual array as representing a single object in motion or in change. The notion of a "correspondence" comes about when the problem is considered (as it is in much of this work) in the context of a sequence of images, such as the frames of a motion picture. The problem then becomes one of establishing a match between parts of one frame and their counterparts in a subsequent frame that represents the same object at a later time.

Once the different views representing the same object have been identified, the next stage is to interpret the changes in the object's appearance in terms of either the motion or the change attributed to the object. The correspondence problem is considered in the first part of this work (Chapters 1, 2, and 3), while the second part (Chapters 4 and 5) examines the 3-D interpretation process.

2. Methodological Comments

1. Discrete presentation: The correspondence problem is considered in most of this work in the context of discrete stimulation, namely a sequence of movie-like frames. The motion perceived under such conditions is called "apparent motion".

> Apparent motion: If two stimuli, such as two bars of light, are presented in a properly timed succession, a clear motion from the first to the second is perceived. Such a motion is also termed "optimal" or "beta" motion. Its occurence depends on several factors, of which timing, spatial separation, and stimuli intensity have been the most extensively studied [Wertheimer, 1912; Korte, 1915; Holvand, 1935; Neff, 1936; Corbin, 1942; Graham, 1965; Kahneman & Wolman, 1970; Attneave & Block, 1973]. The fundamental distinction between "real" and apparent motion is stimulus continuity, not its "reality". In so-called "real motion" the stimulus moves continuously across the retina, while in apparent motion it does not.

Apparent motion conditions provide a framework which is advantageous for studying the correspondence process. On the one hand, the problem becomes simpler since it reduces to the matching of discrete stimuli. On the other hand, there are convincing reasons for believing that apparent and "real" motions are not fundamentally different as far as the correspondence process is concerned [2]. The theory of motion correspondence developed in Chapter 3, as well as that of 3-D interpretation developed in Chapter 4, will be applicable to both types of presentation.

2. The use of demonstrations: Most of the demonstrations in this work were used in much the same way as sentences in the language are used by the linguist. That is, they serve to illuminate points where fine distinctions that call for elaborate psychological experimentation are not required. In several instances (Section 2.5), quantitative measurements were desirable; they were obtained by following standard experimental procedures.

The demonstrations were presented using one of two types of apparatus. One was a DEC GT44 display controlled by a DEC PDP-11/40 computer. The other was a DEC 343 display controlled by a DEC PDP-6 computer. Both devices were connected to a DEC PDP-10 system at the M.I.T Artificial Intelligence Laboratory. A typical presentation was composed of two successive frames. Each frame was shown for a time interval called the *presentation time*, separated by a blank period called the *inter-stimulus interval* (ISI). Unless otherwise specified, the presentation time was 120 msec. and the ISI 40 msec. [3]. All of the displays were observed monocularly in a dimly illuminated room from a distance of about 100 cm. or more [4]. For the experiments in Section 1.2, a Scientific Prototype six-channel stereo tachistoscope was employed. It has a light level of 120 cd/m^2, and a broad band fluorescent light gas discharge. Further details concerning the experiments are described in [Ullman, 1978a].

Nomenclature

Although the terms and abbreviations used are either standard or explained in the text, they are listed here for convenience.

2-D	--	Two-dimensional
3-D	--	Three-dimensional
A(t)	--	The image at time t
AF	--	Affinity
CS	--	Correspondence Strength
ISI	--	Inter-stimulus interval
M.f.S	--	Motion from Structure
msec.	--	Millisecond (1/1000 of a sec.)
S.D.	--	Standard deviation
S.f.M	--	Structure from Motion

PART I

THE CORRESPONDENCE PROBLEM

SYNOPSIS

The correspondence is the process that identifies elements in different views as representing the same object at different times, thereby maintaining the perceptual identity of objects in motion or change. The first three chapters of this work investigate the correspondence process from both experimental and computational approaches. The central messages of Chapters 1 and 2 are that the correspondence process is low-level and autonomous, and that it establishes matches between elementary constituents of images on the basis of a built-in affinity measure and local interactions. Chapter 3 undertakes a computational study of the problem, and develops a workable correspondence scheme which is consonant with the results of Chapters 1 and 2.

Chapter 1. The problem addressed in this chapter is: What are the elements which are matched by the correspondence process?

Section 1.1 argues on theoretical grounds that the correspondence operation should be carried out following the initial organization of the raw visual input into meaningful units. The basic elements, termed *correspondence tokens*, should therefore be such units as edge and line fragments, bars and blobs. The next two sections provide evidence indicating that these are indeed the elements which are matched in the course of human motion perception.

Section 1.2 shows that the correspondence process is not merely an intensity-based operation, thus placing a "lower bound" on the amount of processing that must precede the matching operation.

Section 1.3 examines the "upper bound" problem. It is shown that the correspondence of structured forms is not established between the entire forms on the basis of their similarity, but is built up from matches between small components of the figures.

Chapter 1 thus gives rise to the following view: When motion is established between successive frames, each frame is analyzed up to the level of the correspondence tokens. Correspondence is then established between the tokens via the process discussed in Chapter 2.

Chapter 2 explores the general nature of the correspondence computation and several related issues.

Sections 2.1 - 2.3 examine the principles governing the correspondence, beginning with configurations that are simple enough to avoid being cluttered by abundant interactions. It is shown that a certain similarity measure between correspondence tokens, called *affinity*, is incorporated in the human visual system (Section 2.2). The correspondence between elements is determined from their original affinities via local competition interactions (Section 2.3). These principles are then integrated to form the *competition scheme* for computing correspondence.

Section 2.4 tests the applicability of the competition scheme to various examples. The computed correspondence and its dependence on the ISI (inter-stimulus interval) prove to be consistent with human motion perception. Among the examples considered is the Ternus configuration, which has two modes of perceived correspondence, the "neighbor" and the "coherent" modes. This section draws on the competition scheme to offer an explanation for this bistability, including the transition from the first mode to the second induced by an increase in the ISI.

Section 2.5 examines whether the distance that determines the affinity between correspondence tokens is a two-dimensional, uninterpreted separation, or a three-dimensional, interpreted one. While Chapter 1 gives rise to the expectation that it is the uninterpreted separation, there have been some indications to the contrary based on "smoothness of motion" experiments.

The conclusions of this section are: (1) the correspondence process is governed by the uninterpreted separation; (2) smoothness of motion cannot serve as a measure of the affinity metric.

Section 2.6 suggests that the availability of a low level, autonomous, correspondence process has a potential advantage for other visually related activities. The possibility that the correspondence process plays a role in the early formation of object concepts is discussed. It is suggested that the perception of objects in motion might serve as a basis for, rather than be contingent upon, the concept of a static object.

Chapter 3 is a computational study of the correspondence process. It develops the minimal mapping theory of motion correspondence.

Sections 3.1 - 3.5 define the goal of the process and develop a workable scheme that can accomplish the matching task on the basis of a built-in affinity measure and the local interactions explored in Chapter 2. The scheme, termed the *minimal mapping*, establishes the most probable match between collections of correspondence tokens.

Sections 3.6 - 3.7 compare the minimal mapping with the human correspondence process. Various essential phenomena, including flow detection, symmetry, the minimal cover property, and the multistability of certain configurations, are shown to be derivable from the minimal mapping principle.

Section 3.8 extends the minimal mapping scheme to cover arbitrary correspondence tokens in continuous motion.

Section 3.9 concludes the discussion of the correspondence process by examining some relations between the empirical studies of Chapter 2 and the computational study of Chapter 3.

CHAPTER 1

THE BASIC-ELEMENTS PROBLEM

1.1 Theoretical Considerations

At the core of the capacity to visually perceive motion lies the ability to identify distinct elements in the incoming visual array as representing the same physical object. For a given element X in A(t) (the visual array at time t) its counterpart X' in A(t') (the visual array at a later time t') must be located. X' need not be identical to X in appearance, in fact the very difference between them might serve for the subsequent analysis of the motion, or change, attributed to the object that both X and X' represent.

Before investigating the fundamental correspondence function which matches elements in successive views, we face the more elementary problem of finding the domain and range of this function. That is, what is the set of elements that are mapped in the process of motion perception. I shall refer to the basic elements comprising this set as the *correspondence tokens.* When formulated in terms of the domain and range of a function, this basic elements problem seems misleadingly innocuous. Yet some of the more profound controversies in theories of motion perception stem from a disagreement as to what the basic elements are. Different approaches suggested for the visual analysis of motion have differed in the assumptions they make about the nature of the basic elements. As the particular choice is usually embedded in the theory rather than explicitly stated, it is rarely justified and its implications are seldom discussed. The extreme empiricist view, for instance, suggests that humans learn to associate objects with their different views and are thereby able to recognize these objects in motion. The problem of accepting or refuting this theory is tantamount to the question of whether learned views are indeed the correspondence tokens. Similarly, the controversy of whether or not motion analysis is based upon object recognition is a dispute concerning whether or not recognized objects (or object descriptions) constitute the basic elements of the correspondence function.

The basic elements problem should be the first one considered because of its fundamental importance and the resulting impact it must have on the course of the research. If, for example, object recognition indeed precedes motion analysis, then the correspondence procedure becomes rather simple: the particular element in $A(t')$ corresponding to, say, the white rabbit under the oak tree in $A(t)$, is probably uniquely determined without great difficulty. On the other hand, in such theories of perception, both the correspondence and the three-dimensional interpretation of unfamiliar objects in motion become enigmatic, especially in the case of objects whose two-dimensional views are unrecognizable, as will be discussed in Chapter 4. If, however, the basic elements are more primitive, such as lines, dots, and edge fragments, then familiarity and recognizability cease to play an important role. The correspondence problem then becomes difficult, as there might be many candidates in $A(1')$ for a possible match to, say, a grey line segment in $A(t)$.

The goal of the current section is to suggest, on theoretical grounds, a plausible domain of basic elements. It will be argued that the proper level at which to carry out the correspondence process is that immediately following the initial organization of the raw intensity data into meaningful units. (Meaningful units are, as discussed in the introduction, symbols in the representation whose meanings are founded in the environment, not in the intensity array.) The next two sections provide evidence supporting this view. Section 1.2 shows that organization of the raw intensity data into meaningful units precedes the correspondence operation, while Section 1.3 shows that this antecedent organization is limited to simple, primitive units.

A plausible domain of basic elements

A common approach to picture-matching problems, found in the psychological literature [Kabrisky, 1966; Anstis, 1970; Bell & Lappin, 1973; Pantle & Picciano, 1976] as well as in applications [Leese, Novak & Taylor, 1970; Smith & Phillips, 1972; Wolferts, 1974] is to suggest that the correspondence process takes place prior to any organization of the raw intensity data.

This general view can be further divided according to the particular operation used to establish the correspondence. In one approach [Anstis, 1970] individual points are paired on the basis of their intensity similarity. In this view the role of correspondence tokens is assumed by single intensity points. In more global approaches, a sub-region A of a given intensity array is considered a basic element, and its counterpart A' in a second intensity array is sought on the basis of similarity between their intensity distributions. The similarity of the sub-arrays is usually measured either by a cross-correlation technique, in which maximum correlation is sought, or by subtraction [1.1], wherein the match is indicated by a minimal value.

In the above approaches the correspondence is determined on the basis of similarity between intensity distributions. There are two main arguments against establishing the correspondence by such grey level similarity comparisons.

First, grey level correlations can be expected to yield the correct match only in the very simple case of translation in the image plane. In the general case, in which the two pictures to be compared represent an object in general motion, there is no reason why any of the above grey level comparisons should yield veridical results [1.2]. One of the problems that arises is the "window size" problem. The intensity comparison cannot be performed on single points, nor can it be performed on the image as a whole. The correlation ought to be established between patches of the "right size", but there is no satisfactory way of predetermining that size. The situation becomes even more complex and less amenable to grey level comparisons in the case of several objects which are simultaneously engaged in different motions.

The second objection stems from the fact that grey level distributions and their changes do not correspond directly to physical entities and their motion, while it is the latter that should be established. As illustrated, for instance, by the Cornsweet illusion [Cornsweet, 1970; Ratliff, 1972], a visible edge can have radically different underlying intensity distributions that are perceptually indistinguishable from one another. The Cornsweet illusion should not seem surprising; a given physical edge can, under different illumination and orientation conditions, induce different intensity distributions which by themselves are of no interest to the perceiver who is to recover the physical structure of the environment (c.f. [Marr, 1974; Marr & Poggio, 1976] for the same argument concerning the computation of stereo disparity). Once the edge has been detected, the underlying intensity distribution can be replaced by an edge representation, and a correspondence may then be established between two edge representations. In Section 1.2 the above reasoning will serve to construct a counter-example to the grey level correlation hypothesis.

The foregoing discussion suggests that the discernment of motion should be performed only after the raw intensity data have been organized into units. Such units are probably detected and organized hierarchically, in the sense that units such as edge fragments, bars and small blobs are detected first, then organized into more structured forms, and finally into distinct objects.

If such an organization scheme holds, the appropriate candidates for correspondence tokens are the units situated near the lower end of the hierarchy, (which we shall therefore call *low-level* units). The argument supporting this claim depends in part on the way the correspondence process is carried out and can therefore be fully appreciated only in combination with the discussions in later sections. The gist of the argument, however, is the following. In teleological terms, the problem faced by the visual system in establishing a correspondence is one of guessing the probability that elements X and X' are the same object in motion. It therefore needs some measure of the likelihood that X and X' represent the same object after a slight movement. It is inconceivable that all possible figures are stored in memory together with their likelihood measures, hence this measure must be computed. Only for a certain class of units, namely the members of the basic elements domain, is there indeed a "stored" likelihood measure which we shall call *affinity*. For more complex figures the correspondence is computed from the affinities of their constituents via interactions such as those specified in Section 2.1. The basic elements are therefore expected to be the building blocks out of which complex figures can be structured. The next two sections will support this view by providing evidence that the correspondence is indeed established by matching basic units such as edges, line segments and small blobs. It is of interest to introduce in this context the notion of the *primal sketch* termed by Marr in his theory of early visual processing [Marr, 1976]. The primal sketch is a set of basic units that are the first to be formed in the course of visual analysis, and serve as building blocks for higher-order constructs. From the above discussion it is expected that the domain of correspondence tokens will be roughly equivalent to the elements comprising the primal sketch. This appears indeed to be the case: the two searches for basic units do seem to converge to a similar set of elements.

1.2 The Correspondence is not a Grey Level Operation

The preceding section argued that grey level operations are inadequate for the determination of motion and that organization of the raw data into elementary meaningful units must precede the correspondence process.

In the current section, a demonstration supporting this claim is presented. The demonstration is based on the apparent motion between two pictures. These are designed in such a way that grey level operations imply one kind of motion, whereas a scheme based on pre-organizing the data into meaningful units predicts a different motion.

The intensity profiles of the two pictures used in the demonstration are shown in Figure 1.1 as profiles A and B. Both profiles are derived from graph S in Figure 1.1. Profile A is obtained from S by "smoothing out" the right-hand step, profile B by smoothing out the left-hand step. Perceptually, S contains two sharp edges at positions p and q, while A has a single sharp edge at p, and B a single edge at q. For the subsequent exposition a definition of B's position relative to A is needed. Let the position at which A and B overlap be the 0 position. A positive position will mean that B was displaced to the right, and negative position -- to the left. The entire picture measures 250 units, as indicated in Figure 1.1. Both the position and the intensity units are intended to be on a relative scale only, the actual values can vary within a wide range.

What motion should arise when the two pictures are presented in alternation? If the correspondence is established between perceivable edges the prediction is simple: edges p and q should be seen in motion. If the match is governed by grey level correlation the prediction is different. Graph 1.2a depicts the cross-correlation function between profiles A and B. As seen from the graph, the cross-correlation reaches its maximum at position 0. It is therefore predicted that:

(i) If A and B are shown in registration (position 0) no motion should arise.

(ii) If A is shown first, followed by B displaced by, say, -20 units, then a movement of A by 20 units to the *left* is expected, since a displacement by this amount will maximize the cross-correlation.

The two methods are thus brought into a critical test, predicting opposite results. When the two pictures were presented tachistoscopically, the observed motion was between the visible edges, contrary to the cross-correlation prediction.

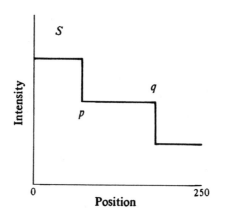

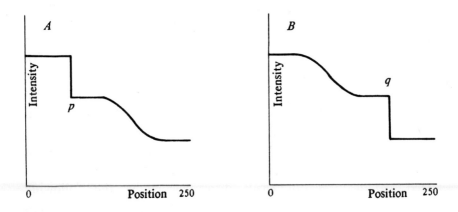

Figure 1.1   Intensity profiles.   Profile *S* gives rise to two distinct edges. Profiles *A* has a single sharp edge at *p*, and *B* a single edge at *q*.

Presentation times were between 100 and 200 msec., with an inter-stimulus interval (ISI) of between 30 and 70 msec. The angular extension of each picture was 3.5 degrees of visual angle, and the separation of the two edges was 1.5 degrees.

Various other grey level operations besides cross-correlation have been suggested for picture comparisons. Graph 1.2b shows the results of applying a second method, called the "subtraction operation" to the profiles in question [1.3]. In this operation, the match is indicated by the minimum value of Graph 1.2b. As with cross-correlation, the match reaches its optimum at position 0. The predictions of the subtraction method are therefore equivalent to those based on the cross-correlation technique, and are likewise rejected by the experimental results. Other grey level operations, such as local correlation (Graph 1.2c) and local subtraction (Graph 1.2d), were examined as well and refuted in a similar manner for the same underlying reason: the changes in the raw intensity distributions do not directly reflect changes in the visible environment. Hence, organization of the visual input into units corresponding to physical entities is a prerequisite for the recovery of physical motion from the changing optical array.

The conclusion that motion correspondence is based on the matching of tokens, not intensity distributions, must be qualified in the case of small displacements by the following comment. There are indications (e.g. the "reversed phi" motion discovered by Anstis [1970], and the short-range process in [Braddick, 1974]) for the existence of a motion detection process that responds to changes in intensity distributions. This process is characterized by its short range (15 - 20 minutes of an arc), and is more effective in peripheral vision, in contrast with the correspondence of tokens that is long range, and effective primarily in central vision. If the two processes do exist, it seems plausible that they might serve different functions. The intensity based peripheral process is adequate for an "early warning system", detecting changes and directing attention. It might also be useful in detecting discontinuity boundaries where

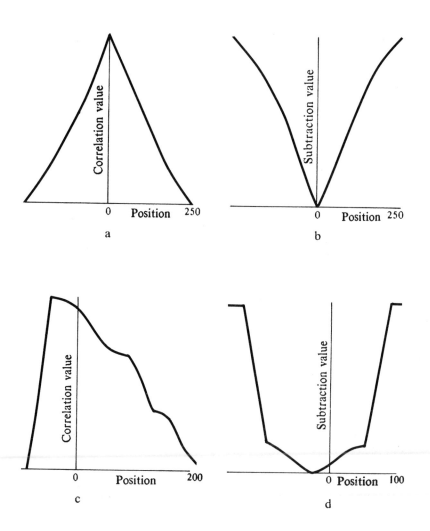

Figure 1.2 Measuring the similarity between profiles A and B of Figure 1.1 (vertical axis) as a function of their position (horizontal axis). In 1.2a global cross-correlation is used, in 1.2b global subtraction process, in 1.2c local cross-correlation, and in 1.2d local subtraction process.

velocities in the visual field change abruptly. The correspondence process, on the other hand, by identifying and tracing tokens, is instrumental in maintaining the perceptual identity of moving objects, and in the 3-D interpretation stage, as will be elaborated in Chapter 4. For the purpose of the present study the possible intensity-based detection process is thus of secondary importance, and will not be discussed further.

In conclusion, the current section places a lower bound on the amount of processing required prior to the establishment of correspondence between image elements. In the next section the upper bound problem is considered. I have argued on theoretical grounds that in the hierarchy of units organized by the visual system, the correspondence tokens are expected to be found at or near the lowest level. The following section provides evidence in support of this view.

1.3 The Correspondence Tokens are not Structured Forms

In this section, five demonstrations will be described in support of the view that the correspondence process does not rely on elaborate form perception. It will be argued that the correspondence perceived between structured forms in motion is not established between the complete forms on the basis of their similarity. Rather, it is the result of a match established between simple constituents of the structured forms. Each demonstration will be described, followed by a brief discussion of the results.

Demonstration 1: The "broken wheel"

The broken wheel display is a modification of a well-known motion picture effect, sometimes called the "wagon wheel" phenomenon, in which a spoked wagon wheel seems to rotate in the direction opposite to its real sense of rotation. This phenomenon indicates the visual system's disposition to choose, from two possible matches, the one which involves minimal change (angular change in this case). As far as the basic

elements problem is concerned the wagon wheel phenomenon admits two different interpretations:

1. The organization of small units into the complete form (the wheel) comes first, and then the form in the first image A(t) is matched against the one found in the later image A(t'). There is more then one way of matching them perfectly, so the one which involves minimum change is selected.

2. Correspondence is established between small sub-units of the wheels, and the motion of the entire form is constructed at a later stage from the motions of the constituents.

In the case of the wagon wheel phenomenon, these two different methods of analysis yield the same result. The "broken wheel" display was constructed in such a way that the two hypotheses would have opposite implications. The rotating figure in this experiment consists of a wagon wheel in which every other spoke is broken, and its middle part is missing (Figure 1.3a). Let α be the angle between two neighboring spokes, and suppose that between successive views the wheel is rotated β degrees counterclockwise. Consider now what happens when $\alpha > \beta > \alpha/2$ (Figure 1.3b; α was 12 degrees and β was 8 degrees). Taking the figure as a whole, a perfect match is achieved by rotating the first wheel β degrees counterclockwise. However, if a short line segment (x in Figure 1.3b) were considered a basic element, and its closest counterpart were sought, then a line segment in the *clockwise* direction (y in Figure 1.3b) might be chosen. Such a choice is impossible according to the first view, but is highly plausible according to the second (though not necessary, for reasons to be discussed in Section 2.4.2). The outcome of the experiment is the following: when appropriately timed, (presentation time of 50 msec. and ISI of 30 msec. in a dark room were required to obtain good, coherent motion), the wheel breaks into three distinct rings. The innermost and outermost rotate clockwise while the middle ring rotates counterclockwise. This breakdown shows that the motion in this case was not established between the complete forms, but between the forms' constituents.

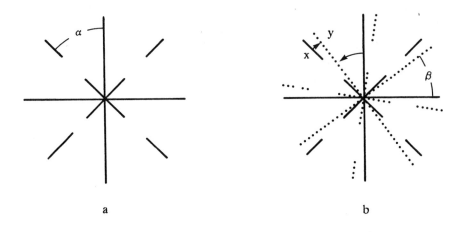

Figure 1.3   The broken wheel demonstration.   Solid lines represent the first frame; dotted lines the second.

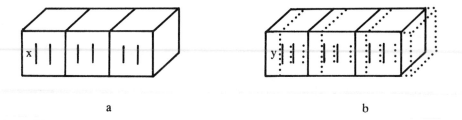

Figure 1.4   The block-train demonstration.   Solid lines represent the first frame; dotted lines the second.

Demonstration 2: The "block train"

The figure in this demonstration is a "block train" comprised of cars with windows as shown in Figure 1.4a. Neighboring vertical lines are separated by x units, and the train moves y units to the right between two successive views (Figure 1.4b). When x/2 < y < x (the actual values employed were x = 0.4 degrees of visual angle, y = 0.3 degrees, with presentation time of 50 msec. and ISI of 30 msec.) there are two principal modes in which the "moving train" is perceived. First, the figure may split: the "windows" move to the left while the rest of the train moves to the right. Alternatively, the entire train may move to the right. The first of the above modes is similar to the broken wheel phenomenon with linear translation substituted for rotation. This mode is seen whenever the viewer fixates at a stationary point on the screen and does not allow his eyes to track the moving train. The second mode is probably the result of eye tracking movements. Suppose the viewer tracks the figure perfectly, that is, the "train" does not move relative to his eye. From the fact that the picture remained unchanged, but eye tracking motions were needed to keep the picture stable, the implication is that the whole figure underwent a translation.

Demonstration 3: The "zebra star"

This experiment involves a rotating star in which every other line is widened (in another version: made longer). Again, let α be the angle between neighboring spokes and β the angle of rotation (Figure 1.5a). If $\beta = \alpha/2$ the zebra star rotates in the direction that will match each wide spoke with a neighboring wide spoke, and each narrow one with its narrow neighbor. If $\alpha > \beta > \alpha/2$ the star is perceived as rotating in the "wrong" direction and at the same time each narrow spoke becomes wider and vice versa.

In the "zebra star" display the figure did not split into sub-units, therefore one might question its significance to the issue in question on the grounds that it can still be explained in

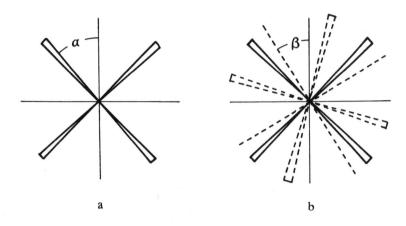

a   b

Figure 1.5 The zebra-star demonstration. Solid lines represent the first frame; dashed lines the second.

terms of the figure as a single unit. The figure as a whole, it might be argued, has two possible matches: a perfect match β degrees away, or another match, closer spatially (α - β degrees), but which implies changes in the figure. One can thus propose the construction of a metric space based on spatial distance as well as on similarity, in which the second match will be "closer" to the original than the first.

This objection is unconvincing for the following reason. The primary advantage of doing form analysis prior to the matching operation is the ability to subsequently identify two figures as corresponding on the basis of figural similarity. One would expect therefore that two complex, identical, and proximate figures should inevitably be matched, a conclusion that runs contrary to the described findings. If complete form analysis does precede the correspondence process one would further expect that a perfect match between complex figures would be a stronger indication of correspondence than a match between small and simple constituents thereof. Experiments with single spokes show, however, that the same ratio β/α is needed both for single spokes and for the whole star, in order to switch the direction of preferred motion.

Demonstration 4: The rotating spiral

In a well-known illusion, a rotating spiral (under either continuous or discrete presentations) seems to expand or contract, depending on its sense of rotation [Kolers 1966]. If the endpoints of the spiral are concealed, only the inward-outward motion is perceived, the rotation is not [Wallach, Weisz & Adams 1956]. The spiral as a whole is involved only in a rotary motion. However, when considering small fragments of the spiral as basic elements, one plausible explanation of the illusion suggests itself. A correspondence between small sub-units of the spiral and their closest neighbors indeed implies a sense of motion perpendicular to the rotation. One can actually observe the outward and inward motion induced by the local correspondence by viewing the display through a narrow radial slit.

Demonstration 5: Correspondence and form

Various attempts have been made in the past to examine the influence that similarity of form exerts on the perceived correspondence between figures. Following the assumption that the matching process should prefer to match similar figures, Kolers [1972] compared the "smoothness" of perceived motion between similar and dissimilar figures. Since the smoothness ratings were found to be the same, independent of figural similarity, Kolers concluded that for the visual system all two-dimensional figures are equally similar. There were, on the other hand, some reports [Orlansky, 1940; Frisby, 1972] that for simple stimuli, especially line segments of different orientations, there were some effects of similarity on the "optimality" of perceived motion.

The findings that similarity between complex forms does not affect their correspondence in any clear way seem to agree with the idea advanced in this section that the matching process occurs prior to the organization of the basic units into structured forms. However, they cannot be accepted as relevant to the problem in question. The main reason is that most of these findings (with the exception of [Navon, 1976] and some demonstrations in [Kolers, 1972]) were based on smoothness of motion judgements which, as shown in Section 2.4, are not a faithful measure of the figures' "tendency to fuse" which they were intended to measure.

A direct method for testing the effect of figural similarity on the matching process is a method which I shall call the *competing motion* technique. In this method two frames are presented in alternation. The first one contains a single element (or figure), while the second frame contains two elements. The question asked is whether the figure in the first frame is seen in motion with one or the other of the elements in the second frame. Figure 1.6a shows an example of a competing motion display. The first frame presents the middle square A alone, while the second frame presents both the outermost square B and the innermost triangle C (presentation time was 120 msec., ISI 40 msec.). The perceived correspondence upon presentation of this display is $A \leftrightarrow B$. That is, the motion between the two squares is preferred. Unlike some past conclusions, these results suggest that figures do differ in their "tendency to fuse". But does this preference indicate an effect of figural similarity? Not necessarily. When the individual lines composing the display are tested in isolation, the preference remains the same. For instance, when x in Figure 1.6a is shown in competing motion with y and z, the motion towards y is preferred. The tendency of square A to fuse with square B rather than with triangle C can thus be explained on the basis of the motion of the constituent elements. There is no need to suppose that the complete forms are the basic elements, nor that a similarity measure between forms determines the observed correspondence. While the correspondence in this example is compatible with both the similarity between the figures and the local match between components, in the next example similarity and local match have conflicting implications.

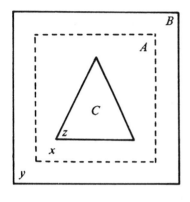

a

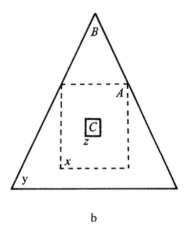

b

Figure 1.6 Correspondence and form. Solid lines represent the first frame; dashed lines the second. In 1.6a the predominant correspondence is between similar forms, in 1.6b between dissimilar ones.

In Figure 1.6b the observed correspondence is between *dissimilar* figures: the preferred match is between the rectangle *A* and the triangle *B* rather than the inner rectangle *C*. Once again, this preference is consistent with the correspondence among constituent elements, e.g. the $x \leftrightarrow y$ match is preferred over $x \leftrightarrow z$. Thus, it is the motion of the constituent elements rather than the similarity between the complete forms that governs the matching process. To sum up the discussion of demonstration 5:

   1. Unlike past conclusions, different figures do
      differ in their "tendency to fuse", but the pref-
      erence is consonant with the motion being

established between their components.

2. There are no indications that structured figures are part of the basic elements domain, or that the correspondence process is based on figural similarity.

All of the demonstrations described above support the claim that no elaborate form analysis must precede the correspondence operation, and that the motion of complex figures is constructed from the motion of their constituents.

Additional support for and elaborations of this view are indicated in two of the subsequent sections. First, the discussion of some relations between the matching process and structured figures is deferred to Section 2.4.2, as they are examined in light of the correspondence scheme advanced in Chapter 2. Second, Section 2.5 shows that the correspondence operation is independent of the three-dimensional interpretation of the scene, thus supporting the view that the correspondence is low level in nature [1.4].

CHAPTER 2

THE CORRESPONDENCE PROCESS

2.1 The General Scheme

2.1.1 Introduction

In Chapter 1, it was concluded that motion correspondence is established by matching elementary tokens. Chapters 2 and 3 address the problem of how this correspondence is established. In this chapter the general principles underlying the matching process are explored. The examination of some simple configurations in motion indicates that the visual system incorporates a certain affinity measure between tokens, which can be roughly considered as a measure of similarity. The correspondence between collections of tokens is derived from the affinities of the tokens via local competition interactions.

A general conclusion that will emerge from Chapter 2 is that the correspondence is a low-level, autonomous process. It depends on spatio-temporal and similarity parameters between elementary tokens in the image, but not on higher level processes such as recognition or 3-D interpretation. Such a low-level, autonomous, correspondence process might explain how disparate views of an object in motion or in change are identified by the visual system as representing a single object. In seeing a moving (or changing) object, the visual system might seem sometimes to transcend the input available to it. A moving or changing object (under discrete presentation) might change drastically in appearance from one frame to the next. However, even when the object is unfamiliar, the visual system is often able to identify the changing views as representing a single object in motion or change. Since the only information available to the visual system is the appearance of the object, it seems puzzling that the system is capable of such identification on the basis of radically disparate views. This capacity is indeed perplexing if the matching is performed on the basis of past familiarity, recognition of the viewed objects, or similarity between complete views. However if the match is established between elementary tokens via the scheme described in the current chapter, then familiarity, recognition, or overall similarity, are not prerequisites for identifying different views as representing the same object.

The possibility that the correspondence between different views is built up from the pairing of elemental sub-units has been rebuked in various ways in the past. Since in my view this approach should be revived, I shall briefly review and criticize the main arguments raised in its denial [2.1].

The correspondence problem gained considerable attention from psychologists of the Gestalt school under such titles as "phenomenal identity" and "selective fusion". In fact, Wertheimer's celebrated 1912 paper [Wertheimer, 1912], which is considered the origin of Gestalt psychology, centered around phenomena of apparent motion, including the correspondence problem. Wertheimer's own work was followed by the studies of Ternus, Metzger, Michotte, Mettelli and others [Koffka, 1935; Vernon, 1966; Ellis, 1967; Arnheim, 1974]. These workers have addressed the problem in a somewhat broader sense than that outlined above, and it is doubtful whether the entire range of phenomena they have considered should indeed be grouped under a single title [2.2]. In the present discussion of the correspondence problem, cases in which object identity is grasped on the basis of conscious reasoning or long term memory comparisons will not be considered.

A major thrust of the Gestalt research into this problem was to demonstrate that the correspondence is established between entire "fields" [2.3], and that it cannot be adequately analyzed in terms of the fields' constituents. The principal argument consisted of constructing examples in which the same element in different fields is paired in dissimilar ways. Figure 2.1 shows some examples. In all of the figures, unfilled circles represent the first of two presentations, while crosses represent the second. (In the actual presentations all of the displayed elements were identical.) A circle filled with a cross means that the element at that position participated in both presentations.

In Figure 2.1a the observed correspondence is $A \to B$ and $B \to C$. In Figure 2.1b, of interest is the correspondence $A \to B$ rather than $A \to A$ [2.4]. Figures 2.1a and 2.1b were taken to demonstrate that the matching process depends more crucially on the "role" of the elements in the field than on spatial proximity. In Figures 2.1c and 2.1e $A \to D$, $B \to E$ etc., while in 2.1d and 2.1f, which are similar to 2c and 2e respectively, D, E, and F correspond to themselves, i.e. they do not appear to move. The Gestaltist's conclusion was that the correspondence function is a function between fields, and that it cannot be further reduced. There is, however, a fallacy in this argument. It is true that the correspondence function is *global* in the sense that changes in one part of the field may affect pairings assigned to elements in some other parts. It does not imply, however, that this function cannot be further decomposed and expressed in terms of simple, local operations. This argument is illustrated schematically in Figure 2.2. In both 2.2a and 2.2b, $\underline{C}$, (which stands for the correspondence function) is an n-valued vector function. Of the "Gestaltron" in 2.2a all one can say is that $\underline{C} = \underline{C}(x_1,.. ..,x_k)$. In 2.2b, $\underline{C} = (f_1,.. ..,f_n)$, where $f_i = f_i(P_i, f_{i-1}, f_{i+1})$. Both functions are global in the sense defined above. In the first case there might not be a simpler way to study $\underline{C}$ then to examine its behavior on different sets of inputs. In the second case, although the "output" anywhere is a function of the "input" everywhere, a simple method for studying and expressing $\underline{C}$ is in terms of the local functions P_i and the interactions f_i. It will be seen in following sections that the latter type of structure indeed seems to underlie the actual correspondence process. The functions were diagrammed in 2.2 as networks, alluding to the point that ultimately they are embodied in some biological structure, and that the locally connected structure in Figure 2.2b is the more likely one. This point will be resumed in Chapter 3.

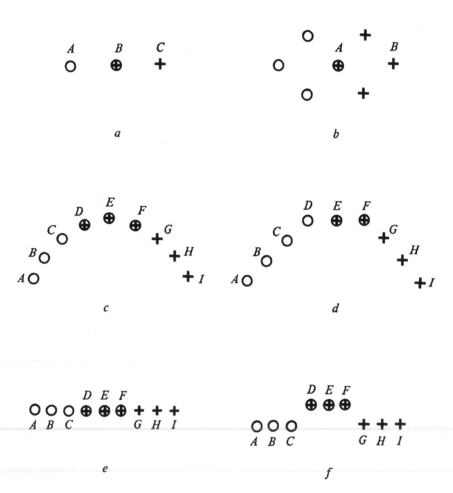

Figure 2.1 Dot configurations used by researchers of the Gestalt school. The first frame is denoted by circles, the second by crosses.

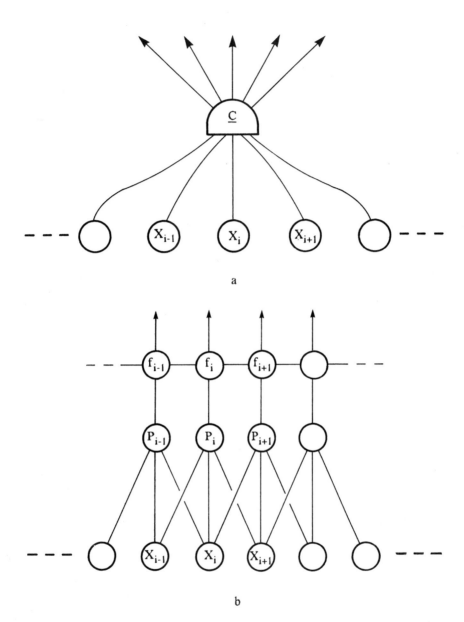

Figure 2.2 A global function computed by a "Gestaltron" (2.2a), and by a local process (2.2b).

Among more recent investigators, Kolers [1972] re-examined the correspondence problem. His finding was that within very broad and hard-to-define limits, every stimulus can be paired with any other one. For example, one character can change smoothly into another, a square can be seen as smoothly transforming into a circle or a triangle, and so on. He then tried to find differences in the "readiness", or "easiness", with which one figure transforms into another. This is a reasonable approach: since a given element X in A(t) can be paired with almost any element X' in A(t'), and since some particular X' is ultimately selected by the visual system, it is reasonable to order the element pairs in a way that would allow for the prediction of the actual correspondence. To achieve this goal, primarily two criteria were used: timing range and smoothness of motion. The timing range criterion is the following. As mentioned in the introduction, the perception of apparent motion depends on the timing of the stimuli presentation. It was probably felt that the stronger a pair's "tendency to fuse", the more tolerant it should be to deviations from the optimal timing [2.5]. It was found, however, that the timing tolerance did not change significantly from one pair of elements to another. The second criterion used was a subjective judgement of the motion's smoothness averaged over many subjects, but again no significant differences were found. Like the Gestalt psychologists, though for different reasons, the systematic analysis of the matching process in terms of basic elements was abandoned.

With the approach that uses smoothness of motion as an indication for the "tendency to fuse" I take issue primarily on methodological grounds. Timing characteristics might reflect some parameters of the system which bear little relevance to the problem at hand. More importantly, as we shall see in Section 2.4, the underlying smoothness assumption is unwarranted: smoothness of motion *cannot* serve as a measure of the "tendency to fuse".

In summary, the Gestalt demonstrations that the correspondence function is global do not preclude its quantitative analysis in terms of simpler, local operations. Attempts aimed at the beginning of such an analysis, in particular the comparisons of the so-called "tendency to fuse" of pairs of elements, did not prove successful, but this failure can be attributed to the employment of inadequate methods. There are, therefore, no strong grounds for discrediting the view suggested by Chapter 1, that motion correspondence is constructed from the matching of elementary tokens.

2.1.2 Affinity and Interactions

The problem to be considered now is the pairing by the correspondence process of tokens in one frame with tokens in the subsequent frame. The investigation will proceed in two stages. If the correspondence between complex figures is built up from the matching of their elementary constituents, a reasonable first step is to examine the correspondence between one or two tokens in isolation. In the second stage, more complex configurations will be examined.

The main result of the first stage (Section 2.2) is that the correspondence between isolated token pairs is governed by a certain "built-in" similarity metric, termed *affinity*. The second stage (Section 2.3) suggests that the correspondence between complex figures is determined from the affinities of their constituents via simple, local interactions.

2.2 Affinity

Displays containing a few isolated tokens reveal a result of fundamental consequence to motion correspondence: different tokens differ in their likelihood to be paired, depending on various parameters of similarity between them. This differential likelihood can be demonstrated and measured using the competing motion technique introduced in Chapter 1. To compare affinities, a certain element, e.g. a dot or a line segment, is shown in alternation with two other elements of the same length, orientation, and separation, one to its right and the other to its left. As a result, two concurrent motions will be perceived. The original line will usually split and participate in motions in *both* directions (Figure 2.3a). Note that the correspondence function in this example is not a one-to-one mapping since the original segment is paired with more than a single element. If one distance is now increased, the likelihood of seeing only one motion (towards the closest neighbor) also increases, until a point is reached where this motion alone is perceived (Figure 2.3b). Thus, matches can differ in the strength

a

b

Figure 2.3 The effect of distance on the affinity between line segments. Solid lines represent the first frames; dashed lines the second.

of their percept, which can be measured by the relative frequency of their being perceived. It should also be noted that split motion is not the only percept associated with the equidistant configuration (although it is by far the most likely, as long as fixation is held at the center). Especially when observed for long periods, one direction of motion might be preferred, and the preferred direction might alternate with time. However, when averaged over time (or over observers) the two directions are of approximately equal likelihood [2.6].

The preference for one match over the other depends not only on the distances, but also on other parameters such as orientation, length, and brightness (or contrast). These preferences suggest that the visual system incorporates an affinity measure that governs the correspondence between isolated tokens. In a correspondence scheme based on the matching of elementary tokens, such an affinity metric is expected to be the primitive operation underlyng the matching process. In this sense the affinity is a "built-in" metric: it is the atomic operation on which the correspondence process is based.

In this section the affinity function will be explored by comparing affinity values between pairs of tokens. Isolated points will be examined first, followed by line segments of various lengths and orientations [2.7]. In the case of isolated points the affinity is shown to be influenced by the distance between the points, and their brightness. Three conditions are examined which affect affinities and therefore must be considered whenever affinities are compared. These include "peripheral increase", "peripheral equation", and "ISI equation".

A straightforward method for comparing affinities is the following. An element X is shown in competing motion with two others, $Y1$ to its right, $Y2$ to its left. It is observed which of the two possible motions is stronger or more probable. A similar but sometimes advantageous method is based on the fact that the affinity functions are monotonically decreasing with distance. When the distance between X and $Y2$ increases, the probability of seeing X in motion with $Y2$ decreases, until at a   particular distance it becomes zero and only the motion towards $Y1$ is perceived. This "null distance" is then compared for different choices of $Y2$'s [2.8]. It should perhaps be noted that the competing motion technique does not provide a direct measure of the affinities involved. As will be discussed in the subsequent section, the affinities in the competing motion situation are modified by competition interactions. However, under reasonable assumptions [2.9], a preferred direction under the competing motion conditions can serve to indicate a higher affinity value.

Consider first the simple situation in which a single point X is shown in competing motion with two other points: $Y1$ at a distance d_1 to one side, and $Y2$ at a distance d_2 to the other (Figure 2.4a; the observer fixates at X). If $d_1 = d_2$ and the points are of the same brightness, X usually splits and moves in both directions. If $d_1 < d_2$ the motion towards $Y1$ prevails, while if $d_2 < d_1$ the motion towards $Y2$ is preferred, and the preference increases as d_2 increases. At distances of $d_1 = 0.5$ degrees of visual angle and $d_2 = 1.5$ degrees (with presentation time of 120 msec. and 40 msec. ISI), the preference towards d_1 is almost total (Figure 2.4b).

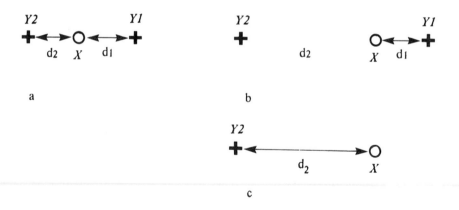

Figure 2.4 The effect of distance on the affinity between dots. Circles represent the first frames; crosses the second. 2.4a: Split motion. 2.4b: Preference for $Y1$. 2.4c: When $Y1$ is removed, X and $Y2$ are seen in smooth motion.

The competing motion displays show one reason why "smoothness of motion" judgements are inappropriate for the study of the correspondence problem. Consider, for example, a configuration in which $Y2$ is at its "null distance", but then remove $Y1$ from the scene. X is immediately seen in a smooth motion with $Y2$ (Figure 2.4c). This result demonstrates the gross insensitivity of the smoothness judgement as a measure of the affinity. Although the affinity of $X \leftrightarrow Y1$ is decisively greater than that of $X \leftrightarrow Y2$, when presented in isolation both pairs are seen in a comparably smooth motion. In Section 2.4 we shall examine another fundamental problem with smoothness judgements, and conclude that smoothness cannot be accepted as a measure of the affinity metric.

A second parameter that affects the affinity besides distance is relative brightness. The effect is not very strong unless the points differ considerably in their brightness, in which case the affinity is stronger between points of similar brightness.

The first and unequivocal conclusion from the above trials is that, contrary to past claims, pairs of basic elements do differ in their affinity. The second conclusion is that the affinity between pairs of points is influenced by both their distance and their relative brightness.

The affinity also varies with the *position* of the display in the visual field, that is, the field is not entirely homogeneous with respect to affinity. The peripheral field differs from the center in two respects:

1. *Peripheral increase.* Affinities increase in strength towards the periphery. This strengthening implies that the point of fixation can have a noticeable effect on the perceived correspondence. If the competing motion configuration described above (Figure 2.4a) is viewed while fixating at $Y1$, the motion $X \rightarrow Y2$ is preferred since $Y2$ is now further to the periphery than $Y1$. Conversely, upon fixating at $Y2$, the affinity $X \rightarrow Y1$ increases in strength, and the motion towards $Y1$ prevails.

2. *Peripheral equation.* A second effect of moving the display toward the periphery is to make the perceived preferences that stem from differences in distance less marked. In other words, the affinities tend to become more uniform towards the periphery. However the preference remains consistent in its sign,

i.e., it does not reverse its direction.

Another condition that influences the affinities is related to the time characteristics of the display, in particular the inter-stimulus interval.

3. *ISI equation.* Increase in ISI has an effect analogous to the peripheral equation, i.e. the preference becomes less noticeable but does not reverse in sign. Increase in the presentation time of the first frame usually has an effect similar to an increase in the ISI [2.10]. (A quantitative measure of the ISI equation in the case of line segments is presented in [Ullman 1978a; graph 1].

The effects of position and timing listed above can be quite noticeable. In experiments concerning affinity it therefore becomes mandatory to pay special attention to the fixation point and the ISI employed.

We turn next to the comparison of affinities between short line segments in isolation.

The affinity between line segments

The parameters discussed above apply to line segments as well as to points, and several additional parameters come into play. We shall first consider the effect of distance on the affinities between line segments, then examine the effects of length and orientation [2.11].

The effect of distance

The affinity between line segments, similar to that between isolated points, depends on their spatial proximity. This dependency is illustrated in Figure 2.5. A single line element c is tested in competing motion with two other segments, l to its left and r to its right. The two flanking segments are parallel to c and of equal length, however l is closer to c than is r. As we have mentioned, the motion towards l is preferred, and the preference grows stronger as the distance between r and c increases.

The effect of proximity is more difficult to assess when non-parallel segments are employed. What, for instance, is the distance in Figure 2.6 between segments c and r? Is it the distance between their midpoints, their terminations, the average separation, or perhaps some other measure? The selection of a specific distance metric is a prerequisite for evaluating the effects of other parameters. Suppose for example that in Figure 2.7 the motion towards l is preferred over the motion towards the shorter segment r. If the distance between the segments' midpoints is considered the relevant distance, the preference might be attributed to the length differences, since r and l are equally distant from c. If the distance is measured differently, e.g. between terminations, then the preference might be attributed, at least in part, to the fact that the c-r distance is now larger than the c-l distance. Consequently, the dependence of the affinity on the length parameter will be weighed differently. A major consideration in selecting a particular metric is that it should yield a simple description of the affinity function. For example, it is desirable that for parallel lines of the same length and brightness the affinity be expressible as a function of the distance alone. This selection criterion can be met, at least approximately, by defining the segments' separation as the distance between their *midpoints*. In Figure 2.8, if midpoint distances are compared, the affinities are expected to be the same, and the observed motion tends to support this expectancy. If, for instance, the minimum distance metric were employed, this equality could not have been accounted for in terms of distances alone. The minimum distance metric is therefore rendered inappropriate by the selection criterion. Other metrics are rejected in a similar manner, while the midpoint measure does seem to obey the selection criterion in most cases, and will therefore be adopted. In addition, most of the configurations used throughout this section were selected in such a way as to minimize the differences between the alternative distance metrics (e.g. Figure 2.9).

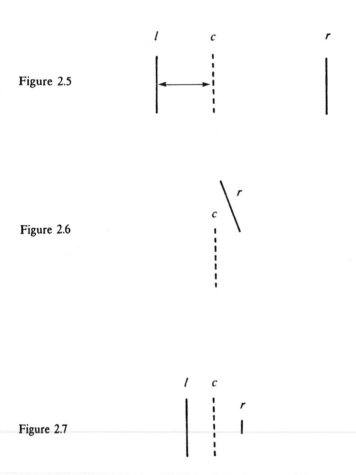

Figure 2.5

Figure 2.6

Figure 2.7

Figure 2.5 - 2.7 Using the selection criterion, the distance between line segments is defined as the distance between their midpoints.

Figure 2.8   Figure 2.9

Figure 2.8   According to the midpoint separation, segments *l* and *r* are equidistant from *c*.

Figure 2.9   In this configuration *l* and *r* are approximately equidistant from *c* according to the various metrics mentioned in the text.

The effect of orientation

The affinity between line segments decreases as a function of the orientation difference between them. Figure 2.9 shows an example in which a segment *c* is tested in competing motion with segments of different orientations. Segment *l* on the left has the same orientation as *c* while *r* on the right does not. The two competing segments are similar in length and brightness and their distances from *c* are the same. Under these conditions the motion towards *l* is preferred, and the preference increases with the angular difference between *c* and *r*.

The effect of length

Similarity of length enhances the affinity between line segments. Other factors being equal, a line segment in competing motion will exhibit a preference for matching the segment which is more similar in length. When segments of different length are matched, a correspondence is usually established between their *termination points* [2.12]. A single line is then seen in motion, changing its length as it moves [Figure

2.10a]. However, when the separation between the segments is sufficiently small, the correspondence of terminations may break down. The shorter segment is then seen in motion with only a *part* of the longer one [Figure 2.10b].

a   b

Figure 2.10 Correspondence between termination points (2.10a), and between a segment and a sub-segment (2.10 b).

Comparing the effects of distance, orientation and length

The relative effects of spatial proximity, orientation, and length on the affinity between line segments were compared using various competing motion configurations.

The results are summarized in Table 2.1 which gives the relative strength of the different effects. For example, it can be seen from the table that the effect of a 60 degrees orientation difference is comparable to the effect of a 2.25 distance ratio or a 2.1 length ratio. All of these entries have a strength of about 3 on a scale of 0 (no preference) to 4 (absolute preference).

Presentation conditions: The central line was about 1 degree of visual angle in length, presentation time was about 120 msec. with 40 msec. ISI, and fixation was

	0	1	2	3	4	
Orientation difference (in degrees)	15	30	45	60	75	90
Distance Ratio	1.1	1.2	1.6	2.25	2.7	3.8
Length Ratio	1.04	1.13	1.5	2.1	2.5	
$1/\cos\alpha$	1.04	1.15	1.41	2.0		

Table 2.1 The relative effect of orientation difference, length ratio, and distance. For details see text.

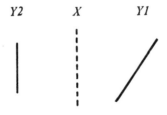

Figure 2.11 According to table 2.1, the effect of 45 degrees orientation differece, and 1.5 length ratio, are equal.

held at the midpoint of the central line. The length
parameter is expressed in terms of a ratio, where one
line always extends one degree of visual angle. Thus,
a length ratio of 2.0 means that one of the flanking
segments was only 0.5 degrees long. Distances are
expressed in a similar way: one segment was kept at
a distance of about 1 degree from the central line,
and the other distance was varied. It is of interest to
observe that within the experimental conditions the
actual lengths were of little importance, the ratio
being the relevant parameter. If, for example, a 30
degrees tilt offsets a distance ratio of 1.2, then this
relation holds for a wide range of line lengths [2.13].
The results are averaged over two observers, each
making ten judgements per configuration. It should
be noted that these results were obtained for
presentation times of 100 msec. and longer, viewed at
the center of the visual field. There are some
indications that the affects of orientation and length
might depend on the presentation time, as well as on
position in the visual field.

Examples of using the diagram: X will denote the central line
segment in the first presentation (always vertical), Y1 and Y2
compose the second presentation.
(a) Y2 is tilted by 60 degrees from the vertical, Y1 is vertical.
Y1 is preferred by 3, namely a "considerable preference".
(b) Y1 is tilted by 45 degrees while the length of X is 1.5 that
of Y2. The diagram shows that there is no preference, the two
motions will be equally probable (Figure 2.11).

As can be seen from the table, the affinity of line
segments is related to the similarity between them. A further
point of interest is the relation between the relative effects of
orientation difference and length ratio. Consider two views of a
line segment that is at first parallel to the image plane, and then

rotates by α degrees. If the rotation takes place in the image plane, then the resulting two segments (before and after the rotation) have the same length, but differ in orientation by α degrees. If the segment is rotated *in depth*, it does not change its orientation, but only decreases in length. The ratio of the original to final length (ignoring perspective effects) is $1/\cos\alpha$. If the initial orientation of the segment is not parallel to the image plane, the same relation holds, provided that the angle of rotation α is sufficiently small. Table 2.1 reveals that the effects of an orientation difference of α degrees and length ratio of $1/\cos\alpha$ are comparable (up to roughly 75 degrees). Thus, the affinity measure is consistent with a measure of orientation differences *in space*. In an image of an object rotating in space, the correspondence pattern is thus expected to be similar whether the object rotated in depth or in the plane. The experiments with rotating figures of Shepard and Judd [1976] might be of relevance to this point. They found that a breakdown in the coherent correspondence between images of a rotating figure occured for the same rotations in depth and in the image plane.

2.3 Higher Order Interactions

2.3.1 Split and Fusion Competitions

When compound displays containing a larger number of tokens are examined, the correspondence pattern can no longer be accounted for on the basis of affinity alone. As we shall see, the original affinities are modified by inter-element interactions, so that the match assigned to a given element is no longer necessarily its highest affinity neighbor. The role of the affinity function is thus analogous to that of the elemental functions P_i in Figure 2.2b, with the higher-order interactions we are about to examine playing the part of the functions f_i. To distinguish between the initial affinities and the final correspondence pattern, I shall introduce the notion of *correspondence strength*, abbreviated as CS. In a compound display, if the match of an element x with element y is preferred over the match with z, we shall conclude that $CS(x,y) > CS(x,z)$ (i.e. the CS between x and y is higher than the CS between x and z). If $CS(x,z) = 0$, they will never be seen in motion [2.14].

The objective of this section, which is the examination of the correspondence in compound configurations, can now be stated in terms of the CS: we wish to find a method of computing the CS on the basis of the initial affinities. The main outcome of this section is that the CS is derived from the affinities between tokens via simple, local interactions. The significance of this outcome is twofold. First, it supports the result of Chapter 1 that correspondence in general is based on the matching of elementary tokens. Second, it will be instrumental in the development of a computational theory of correspondence in Chapter 3. In this section I shall discuss two types of interactions, which I shall term *split competition* and *fusion competition*. The subsequent section will combine the results concerning affinity and interactions into a single framework, called the *competition scheme*. In Section 2.4 the competition scheme will be applied to several examples, to show that the correspondence is indeed consistent with the competition scheme.

In competing motion, a single element X is shown in alternation with two other elements, $Y1$ and $Y2$. The resulting back-and-forth motion of the elements is composed of two phases, split and fusion, which will now be examined separately. In the split phase a single element X is replaced by a pair of elements $Y1$ and $Y2$. In the fusion mode the pair of elements are presented first, followed by the single element. Each phase can be studied on its own, using a tachistoscopic mode of presentation. That is, one shows the two frames in rapid succession, followed by an inter-sequence interval of a few seconds. If X is shown first, followed by $Y1$ and $Y2$, only the split phase of the motion is observed. To study the fusion phase the order of presentation is reversed: $Y1$ and $Y2$ are presented first, followed by X alone.

Split competition: We have already seen that in the competing motion situation (Figures 2.3 and 2.4) the motion between X and $Y2$ breaks down in the presence of another element $Y1$ sufficiently close to X. The same phenomenon holds for each of the phases separately. If X is presented followed by $Y2$ alone, X is seen to move and match $Y2$. In the presence of $Y1$, however, only the $X \rightarrow Y1$ motion is seen. This breakdown implies that owing to the competition, the final value $CS(X,Y2)$ is less then the original affinity $AF(X,Y2)$. The situation is probably symmetric [2.15], that is $CS(X,Y1) < AF(X,Y1)$. Figure 2.12 illustrates this situation schematically. The final CS between X and $Y1$ depends on both $AF(X,Y1)$ and $CS(X,Y2)$, and similarly for the CS between X and $Y2$. More generally, the correspondence strength $CS(A,B)$ between two given elements A and B is reduced by split competitions from any other element Z for which the $CS(A,Z)$ is non-zero.

Fusion competition: When the fusion phase of the competing motion is isolated, the same breakdown effect holds. The motion $X \leftarrow Y2$ breaks down in the presence of $Y1$. The effects of split and fusion competition seem to be of equal strength, namely, the effect of $Y1$ on the perceived motion between X and $Y2$ is about the same in both phases. As a second example of fusion competition in a slightly more complex situation, consider Figure 2.13a versus 2.13b. In 2.13a $X1$ is seen as splitting and moving in both directions. In 2.13b on the other hand $X1$ is involved in one motion only, to the right. It is as if $X2$ (which might be on either side of $Y2$), by taking hold of $Y2$, prevents the correspondence $X1 \rightarrow Y2$. This means that $AF(X2,Y2)$ reduces $CS(X1,Y2)$, that is, $CS(X1,Y2) < AF(X1,Y2)$ because of the interaction.

The two kinds of competitions are illustrated schematically in figure 2.14. The full arrows indicate a non-zero affinity between the two elements. The dashed arrows indicate competition: the horizontal represent split competition, the vertical represent fusion competition. *A1* may match *B1*, *B2* or *B3*, hence they all interact via split competition. A similar

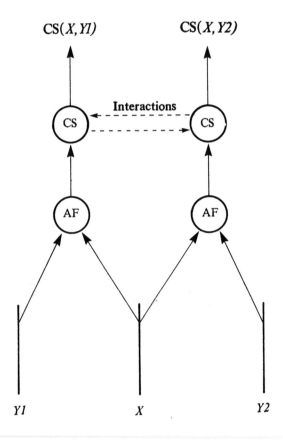

Figure 2.12   The CS is derived from the underlying affinities via local interactions.

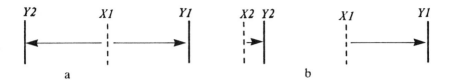

Figure 2.13 Fusion competition. In 2.13a *X1* splits. In 2.13b it does not, due to fusion competition from *X2*.

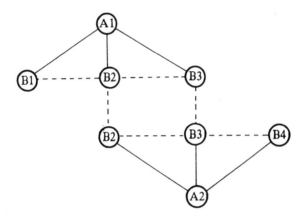

Figure 2.14 A diagram combining split and fusion competitions.

situation holds for the matches between *A2* and *B2, B3, B4*. Both *A1* and *A2* have *B2* and *B3* as possible matches, hence these matches interact through fusion competition. Although the current state of knowledge defies serious attempts to correlate the above functions with known physiological structures, **Figure 2.14** suggests a possible general scheme for such a network in which the full arrows stand for facilitation, the dashed ones for competition. We shall further address this point in **Chapter 3**.

2.3.2 The Competition Scheme

The examination of simple displays has revealed several guidelines that underlie the correspondence process. I shall call the
scheme that integrates all the principles outlined so far the
competition scheme for computing correspondence. The competition scheme is not completely determined since the exact form of
the affinity and interaction functions is not yet known. For the
sake of clarity, the principles incorporated in the competition
scheme are recapitulated below.

1. *Affinity:* There is an affinity measure between pairs of
motion tokens which depends primarily on the distance between
them, various similarity parameters, timing parameters, and
viewing conditions. The similarity parameters include
brightness, orientation and length. The effects of timing and
viewing conditions are summarized in the next three items.

2. *Peripheral increase:* The affinity increases in strength towards
the periphery of the visual field.

3. *Peripheral equation:* Differences between affinities are less
noticeable in the periphery compared with the center of the
visual field.

4. *ISI equation:* increase in the ISI has the effect of making the
affinities more uniform, thereby masking correspondence
preferences.

The eventual correspondence strength is derived from the
underlying affinities via two kinds of competitions which are
stated next.

5. *Split competition:* If a given token has several possible
matches, all those with non-zero correspondence strength
compete with one another.

6. *Fusion competition:* If several tokens have a common element
as their possible match, all matches with non-zero CS compete
with one another.

The next section will test the competition scheme by
applying it to configurations that are more complex than the

ones from which it has been derived.

2.4 Application of the Competition Scheme to Examples

In the preceding sections a competition correspondence scheme has been developed by combining several rules that govern the correspondence process in simple displays. It is, of course, possible that additional rules participate in determining the matching process. However, it seems methodologically advisable to adopt a conservative attitude and to refrain from introducing new rules (unless the competition scheme is manifestly insufficient), thereby avoiding the confusion that might otherwise result from the proliferation of unwarranted rules.

In this section the competition scheme is applied to several examples to test its sufficiency in more complex situations. The correspondence that is actually perceived is shown to be in accord with the competition scheme even in some cases that were considered challenging to motion perception theories [Kolers, 1972; Attneave, 1974]. The goal is to show that these seemingly troublesome cases are in fact consistent with, and predicted by, the competition correspondence scheme. Four cases will be examined by comparing the perceived correspondence with the results predicted by a particular version of the competition scheme (more examples may be found in [Ullman, 1977a]). By using a particular version, I mean that some specific affinity and competition functions have been chosen. Since sufficient data are not yet available for determining the actual shape of these functions, detailed experimentation with a particular model is premature. However, the point is to demonstrate that the examples *can* be accounted for by a competition scheme and therefore no additional interactions need be hypothesized on the basis of these examples. The competition scheme used in this section is detailed in [Ullman, 1977; Appendix 4].

2.4.1 Four examples

Each of the following examples was composed of two frames shown in apparent motion. Each frame presented either a single element (a small blob extending about 12 minutes of visual angle) or a number of elements lying in a horizontal row [2.16]. For convenience of illustration, the second presentation is drawn underneath the first, although they were actually all in a line. The elements of the first presentation are denoted by *A1, A2*, etc., the elements of the second presentation by *B1, B2*, etc. The numbers labelling the links between pairs of elements represent the affinity or the CS between the two elements. Each of the examples is accompanied by three figures. The first shows the original affinities used in the computation. These affinities (described in [Ullman, 1977; Appendix 4]) were chosen to conform with the rules of the competition scheme. Two types of affinity functions were used. The first, referred to as the "neighbor mode" condition, tested short ISI, and central viewing. The other, called the "coherent mode" condition (see below), is obtained from the first by making the affinities more uniform. The second figure in each example presents the final correspondence strengths which result from the combined effect of the affinities and the competition interactions. The third figure illustrates the actually perceived correspondence. Since some matches are perceived more frequently than others, the following notation is used. Full arrows represent strong, stable matches, while dotted arrows denote a correspondence that is weaker and less stable. Most of the displays used configurations tested by Kolers [1972] [2.17].

Example 1: Three-way split

Splitting motion is not restricted to pairs of elements. Three-way splits were examined by Kolers [1972], and an example is illustrated in Figure 2.15. In agreement with actual perception, the competition scheme indicates a preference for the closest neighbor which diminishes at long ISI. When observed under short ISI conditions, *B0* and *B2* (the right and left elements) do not appear to move. At longer ISI all three elements are seen in motion, however the motion between *A* and *B1* remains the strongest.

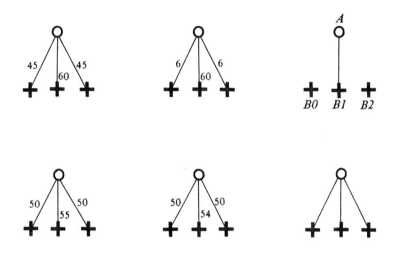

Figure 2.15   Three-way split. At short ISI the nearest neighbor is strongly preferred (2.15a). At longer ISI a split is observed.

Example 2: "Ternus' configuration"

This example will be considered in some detail since it exhibits an interesting dependence on the ISI employed, and since it has been used as an argument against founding the correspondence process on basic elements [Ternus, 1926]. The display in this example contains two elements in each frame: elements *A1* and *A2* in the first frame, *B1* and *B2* in the second [2.18]. The elements can be either points or parallel line segments, and the positions of *A2* and *B1* coincide, as shown in Figure 2.16. Depending (among other parameters) on the distances and ISI

A1   *A2*

B1   *B2*

Figure 2.16 Ternus' configuration. Circles represent the first frame; crosses the second. (In the actual presentation all three elements were identical.)

used in the display, one of two modes of correspondence is perceived. In the first mode *A1* is paired with *B1* and *A2* with *B2*, that is, the pair moves "as a whole" to the right. I shall refer to this mode of perceived motion as the *coherent mode*. In the second mode the correspondence is *A2* → *B1* (that is, *A2* is paired with *B1)* and *A1*, if seen to move at all, is paired with *B2*. The element *A2* is paired in this case with its closest neighbor, and I shall therefore refer to this kind of perceived correspondence as the *neighbor mode*. The Gestalt argument [Ternus, 1926; Koffka, 1935] interpreted the coherent mode, in which *A2* is not paired with its closest neighbor *B1*, as indicating that the counterpart of *A2* is established according to its "role in the field", implying that complete "fields", not isolated elements, constitute the correspondence tokens [2.19]. But the observed correspondence is actually in agreement with the competition scheme outlined above. Although *B1* is *A2*'s closest neighbor, the competition interactions might still cause the eventual match to be *A1* → *B1*, *A2* → *B2*. To see why, remember that the final correspondence strength between two elements depends on both the initial affinity between them and the interactions that reduce the correspondence strength. Thus, although the affinity between

A2 and *B1* is certainly stronger than the affinity of *A2* → *B2*, the competing interactions might render the final CS of *A2* → *B1* *weaker* than the CS between *A2* and *B2*. The question of which mode of correspondence will be perceived under given conditions cannot be settled without knowing both the affinities and the interactions involved. Qualitative prediction can, however, be made. It is expected, for instance, that for fixed ISI the coherent correspondence mode will predominate at small inter-element distances (distance *d* in Figure 2.16), and the neighbor mode at large distances, as is indeed the case [2.20].

      The competition scheme, based on the interactions inferred from simpler cases, is sufficient to explain, at least qualitatively, the observed correspondence in Ternus' configuration as well. The explanation is more complete than the "field" description since it predicts the dependency of the observed mode on the inter-element distance. Methodologically, it seems undesirable to resort to any new interactions or organizational rules unless the two competition interactions are shown to be insufficient.

The affect of ISI on Ternus' configuration

      Various factors are able to induce a transition in Ternus' configuration from one mode of perceived correspondence to the other. For example, under dichoptic presentation (i.e. one frame is shown to one eye, the second to the other) the coherent mode prevails [Pantle & Picciano, 1976]. Among other parameters that affect the perceived mode are the inter-element distances, the relative intensity of the different elements, and the ISI. The ISI effect is that for short ISI the neighbor mode of Ternus' configuration prevails, while at long ISI the coherent mode takes over. A gradual increase in the ISI will cause a fairly sharp transition from the neighbor to the coherent mode [Pantle and Picciano 1976].

      The effect of increase in ISI is not limited to the two-dot Ternus configuration. Pantle and Picciano [1976] observed the same transition between modes using a three element display.

Similar modes can be observed in random dot displays, composed of two frames. The first frame is comprised of points scattered randomly across the screen. The second frame is of the same collection of points, displaced as a whole by a given amount. At very short ISI the tendency is to observe local, unrelated motions. At longer ISI the coherent mode increases in strength, i.e. the tendency to see a uniform translation of the entire collection increases. Pantle and Picciano [1976] who studied the mode transition phenomenon concluded that it occurs at an ISI of about 40 msec. However, this finding is not universal. That is, different configurations differ in the ISI at which the transition to the coherent mode occurs. In Ternus' configuration, for instance, the larger the inter-element distance, the longer the ISI required for the transition.

A possible explanation: ISI equation

The transition to coherent mode as the ISI increases is predictable from the competition scheme. There is no need to conjecture additional mechanisms, or to propose the existence of "two separate systems" [Pantle & Picciano, 1976]. We have seen that the ISI can affect the correspondence process via the ISI equation. It was mentioned that the affinity between basic elements depends on the ISI such that at longer ISI the affinities tend to become uniform in strength. As we shall now see, within the framework of the competition scheme, the phenomenon of the ISI equation can cause a transition from neighbor to coherent mode. The results of applying the competition scheme to Ternus' configuration at short ISI is compared in Figure 2.17 to the limiting case of coherent mode conditions where all the affinities are equal. In the short ISI condition the affinity of $B \to B$ is the strongest. Via competition effects it weakens, and practically nullifies, the links $A \to B$ (fusion competition) and $B \to C$ (split competition). The link $A \to C$ (not shown) is unaffected and remains equal to the original affinity. Under the long ISI condition the combined competition of the $A \to B$ and $B \to C$ links is sufficient to nullify the link $B \to B$, and consequently the coherent mode prevails. Furthermore, the competition scheme exhibits the same bistable behavior that characterizes the perception of Ternus' configuration. As the increase in ISI gradually equalizes the affinities, there is a rather sharp transition from a complete dominance of the neighbor mode to a complete dominance of the coherent mode.

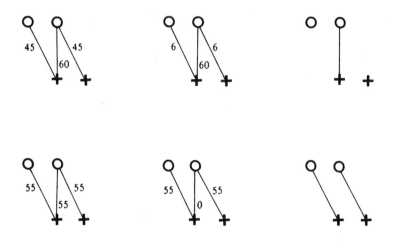

Figure 2.17 Ternus' configuration under short ISI (top row) and long ISI conditions (bottom row).

If the above analysis is correct and the ISI equation is indeed responsible for the coherent mode, the following prediction can be made. Since translating the display towards the periphery has an analogous effect to increasing the ISI, viewing Ternus' configuration off the center of the visual field should enhance the coherent mode. This prediction can be verified by comparing the perceived motion while fixating at the center of the display versus fixating 1.5 degrees above the center.

As expected, the coherent mode is enhanced in the second case.

The above presentation is somewhat over-simplified. Additional complications arise as a result of higher-order grouping, as discussed in the second part of Section 2.4.2, and the short-range effect mentioned in Section 1.2. Some additional aspects of Ternus' configuration will be examined in light of the theoretical considerations in Chapter 3.

Mode transition and saccadic suppression

The eyes are constantly engaged in various types of motion, one of which is called *saccades*. A saccade is a ballistic motion of the eyeball. Saccades happen on the average about twice per second, they are fast, and usually of a rather large amplitude (about five degrees on the average for voluntary saccades) [Davson, 1969; Ditchburn, 1973].

A curious effect associated with saccades is the phenomenon called *saccadic suppression*. Not surprisingly, visual acuity during the saccade itself, when the image sweeps rapidly across the retina, is severely impaired [Volkman, 1962]. Less expected is the fact that this loss of clear vision is considerably longer than the saccade itself: it starts about 40 msec. *prior* to the saccade, and outlasts it by about 50 msec. [Mackay, 1970; Ditchburn, 1973]. This loss of acuity during saccades is termed *saccadic suppression*. It results in an increase in the time interval during which vision is impaired from 25-40 msec. to over 100 msec. per saccade. In other words, at a rate of 4 saccades per second, visual acuity is impaired for about 50% of the time.

One might suppose that the existence of saccadic suppression is an unfortunate corollary of some properties of the ocular system. However, Mackay [1970] demonstrated that saccadic suppression exists even *without* any motion of the eyeball. If instead of moving the eye the image is rapidly shifted across the retina, the decrease in visual acuity follows much the same pattern as in the actual saccade. It is as if the visual system, whenever confronted with a large, rapid displacement, suppresses visual information within a time span of about 100 msec. [2.21].

The discussion concerning the two modes of perceived correspondence raises the possibility that saccadic suppression serves a useful purpose in overcoming a problem that arises from large, rapid displacements of the retinal image. I have mentioned that the *distance* between elements plays a major role in determining the correspondence. The shorter the distance, the higher the affinity. Consequently, elements tend to match their nearest neighbors. Such a neighbor mode of correspondence is expected to be useful only as long as the rate of motion is reasonably small. If, for instance, a motion picture is taken of elements in rapid motion, there is no guarantee that a given element in one frame can be correctly identified with its nearest neighbor in the successive frame. The conclusion is that whenever the displacement of the retinal image between successive "snapshots" is large, the neighbor mode is likely to produce *accidental matches.* A plausible solution is to switch under these conditions to a coherent mode, in which a common displacement of the elements is sought. We have seen that such a switch from neighbor to coherent mode is caused by an increase in the ISI. An average saccade can be thought of as two "snapshots" separated by an ISI of reduced, blurred vision that lasts about 25-40 msec. This interval is often still within the neighbor mode domain. A possible method for forcing a switch to the coherent mode is to increase the interval of impaired vision beyond the time of the actual saccade. It is also useful to exert the same suppression upon detecting a sudden, rapid displacement of the image.

Our knowledge of the so-called saccadic suppression is still scant, and the above suggestion is necessarily speculative. However, if it is in the right direction, and if saccadic suppression is indeed the manifestation of some useful process, attention should shift from the search of possible linkages which happen to connect eye motions with impaired acuity, to such problems as methods for detecting rapid displacements, and for controlling visual acuity.

Example 3: Non-symmetric motion

The configuration used in this example is shown in Figure 2.18. Although the configuration is symmetric, the perceived correspondence is usually asymmetric: the central element $A2$ moves either to the right or to the left, giving rise to a bistable configuration. Infrequently, the correspondence assumes a symmetric pattern, and the central element does not move at all, or (very rarely) splits and moves in two directions. The symmetric motion arises in the competition scheme when the original affinities of $A2 \to B1$ and $A2 \to B2$ are exactly the same (top row). Due to the interactions, the CS of both links becomes very small, and they might not survive at all. If the original affinities of $A2$ are not exactly the same, then usually the stronger one survives the competition (bottom row). The conclusion is that the symmetric match is possible, but unstable and therefore unlikely. Figure 2.18 shows the resulting CS (under short ISI) for both the symmetric and non-symmetric cases.

Example 4: Symmetric motion

Three elements in a row are presented in alternation with four other elements (Figure 2.19). Unlike example 3, the middle element here does participate in a split motion. Global symmetry principles have been invoked to explain this display [Attneave, 1974]. However, no principles beyond the local competition scheme are required. The CS as computed by the scheme implies exactly the motion pattern which is actually perceived.

The above examples support the view that motion correspondence is derived from the initial affinities by simple, local interactions. The competition scheme can reasonably account for the observed behavior of the correspondence process in the tested configurations, under short and long ISI conditions. Although the actual values produced by the scheme depend on the particular functions employed, the qualitative behavior (i.e. the patterns of preferences) is determined primarily by the competition scheme's basic properties. That is, the functions can

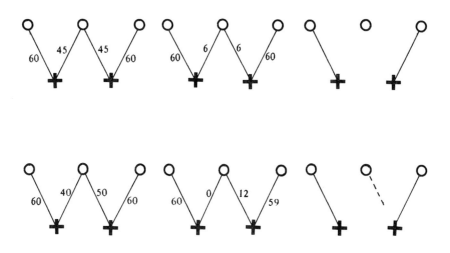

Figure 2.18 Non-symmetric motion.

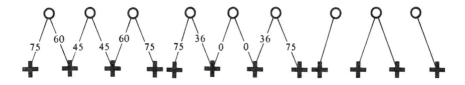

Figure 2.19 Symmetric motion.

be changed within a wide range without having major effects on the predicted correspondence [Ullman, 1977a; Appendix 4].

2.4.2 Organization into Higher Order Units

In this section an example will be presented for which the competition scheme fails when applied to the individual elements in the display. The scheme does succeed, however, if a plausible extension of the motion tokens domain is made.

Consider the display shown in Figure 2.20a and b. In 2.20a a small line segment C is shown in competing motion with segments L and R. In 2.20b each line segment is replaced by a pair of points at its end points. The competition correspondence scheme, when applied to the individual points in 2.20b predicts that the matches $C1 \to L1$, $C2 \to R2$ will predominate. The perception associated with the display does not confirm this prediction. The two points $(C1, C2)$ do not separate. They sometimes move to the left to match the pair $(L1, L2)$, and sometimes to the right to match $(R1, R2)$. Occasionally, these motions are perceived simultaneously. The modes of perceived motion and their relative strength are in agreement with display 2.20a which uses line segments instead of point-pairs.

The competition scheme fails to predict the correct results when applied to the individual points. The example suggests that under the displayed conditions each pair of points was considered by the correspondence computation as equivalent to a short line segment. The fact that a proximate pair of points is treated by the correspondence process as a short line segment need not seem strange. I have argued in the first chapter that the correspondence is established between tokens which constitute the building blocks of structured figures, such as bars, edges and blobs. Contours, boundaries, and texture elements are detected by the visual system in a variety of ways. One such method is the grouping of nearby points, or more

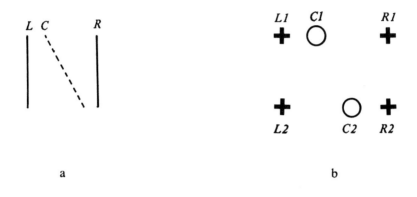

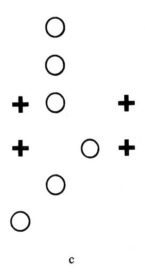

Figure 2.20 Group tokens. The dot pairs in 2.20b behave like the line segments in 2.20a. In 2.20c the background dots disrupt the grouping effect.

generally "place tokens" which satisfy certain conditions [Marr, 1976]. Another possible method is to detect the boundary between regions of different textures, and there is a report [Ramachandran *et al*, 1973] that motion can be established between such edges. Correspondence can also be established under the appropriate conditions between two fuzzy blobs, or "clouds" of numerous small elements, without necessarily establishing a match between the individual elements. A study by Julesz and Payne [1968] indicates that disparity boundaries in random dot stereograms can serve as motion tokens as well. Edges, lines, blobs, and other elementary tokens detected in some or all of the possible ways might belong to the level proposed in the first chapter for carrying out the correspondence operation. Such a grouping was, therefore, to be expected, but its examination had to await the elaboration of the competition scheme. Without the development of the scheme it is difficult to argue for the existence of grouping, since it is unclear whether or not the observed correspondence can be explained without resorting to grouping. For example, unlike Figure 2.20b, most of the Gestalt demonstrations do not really imply the existence of any organization at all, since they can be explained by the competition scheme alone (e.g. Figures 2.1a and 2.1b, while figure 2.1d and 2.1f might be the result of grouping). The motion of the elements in 2.20b depends on their being grouped into a unit, and not on a simple proximity criterion alone. For example, in the configurations shown in Figure 2.20c the two points only rarely move together, since they are no longer grouped into the same token. An alternative way of disrupting the effect of grouping is to reduce the presentation time of the first frame. However, a short presentation time has the undesirable effect of making the motion harder to perceive.

Basic elements which are formed by the grouping of other basic elements will be called *group tokens*. An important property of the group tokens is that they do not replace their constituents. Rather, they are added to the set of possible matches, competing with the correspondences between the constituents but not excluding them. If the CS between the individual components is sufficiently large it might dissolve the group token. This holds for line segments (see the "broken wheel" demonstration in Section 1.3) as well as for rows of dots, and the denser the row, the more resistant it becomes to disintegration. The exact nature of the interactions between the correspondence of group tokens and the matching of their constituents remains to be clarified. For example, it is not yet clear whether high CS between groups can reinforce in any way the CS between constituents thereof.

The following statements summarize the discussion of higher order elements.

1. The basic elements domain includes group tokens. It has been argued that this is a plausible assumption, which explains the similarities between displays 2.20a and 2.20b.
2. The group tokens can be constructed by grouping elements into simple units such as line segments and probably blobs and edges. Unlike the Gestalt "field" notion, there are no indications for higher organization into structured forms (and there are indications to the contrary, see Chapter 1).
3. The group tokens are added to the domain of basic elements; they do not replace their constituents. Consequently, the group might move as a whole but might also break down into independent motions of the constituent elements.

The grouping phenomenon raises a question concerning the mode transition in Ternus' configuration. Can the transition to the coherent mode be the result of grouping the points into a single line segment? Indeed, the effect of both grouping and ISI equation is to strengthen the coherent mode, and thus either phenomenon might be responsible for the mode transition. It can be shown, however, that the ISI equation by itself is probably sufficient to cause the transition. To test this claim, additional background dots can be added to the display to disrupt the grouping, as was done in Figure 2.20c with respect to 2.20b. Figure 2.21 shows an example of applying this procedure to Ternus' configuration. The squares stand for the background elements; they participate in both the first and second frames (in the actual presentation all elements were identical in shape). In this configuration, elements *A*, *B*, and *C*, exhibit the same transition between modes as the standard Ternus configuration.

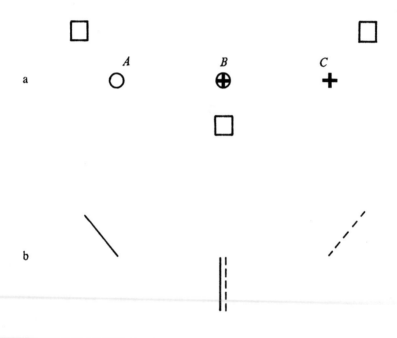

Figure 2.21a Ternus' configuration accompanied by background elements (denoted by squares). 2.21b is derived from 2.21a by substituting line segments for pairs of proximate dots.

If the match were established between group tokens, the grouping would be expected to assume the form of 2.21b: proximate elements are grouped into lines (full lines depict the first frame, dashed lines the second). When the line configuration in 2.21b is actually tested in motion, the correspondence (for short ISI) is predominantly $A \rightarrow B$, which is different from the match in 2.21a. The conclusion is that grouping is not required for the mode transition in Ternus' configuration to take place. It is still possible, however, that grouping might contribute to transitions between modes in the Ternus as well as in other configurations. It seems to me that grouping processes are of particular importance, and that they should be among the main areas to explore in further studies of the correspondence process. Some other problems that will require further investigation are the experimental determination of the affinity and the interaction functions. In pursuing the inquiry into various aspects of the correspondence process it seems profitable to proceed from universal aspects to more particular details. Following this guideline, the next section raises a general issue concerning the relation between the correspondence process and the three-dimensional interpretation of images.

2.5 Affinity and Three Dimensional Interpretation

2.5.1 Affinity and Distance

A parameter that plays an important role in the determination of the affinity between elements is the distance between them. In this section the following question is posed: what kind of spatial separation affects the affinity; is it only the uninterpreted, two-dimensional distance, or is it influenced by the interpreted three-dimensional separation?

In the course of visual analysis, figures are usually given a three-dimensional (3-D) interpretation which affects the judgment of spatial relations between figure constituents. The resulting percept is often biased by both the 2-D and the interpreted 3-D relationships, as exemplified in Figure 2.22. Segment R in Figure 2.22 appears to lie *above* C and *below* L.

In 3-D space C and R are on the same level if the direction of C and R is taken to represent the vertical dimension. In the 2-D picture plane, R and L are exactly symmetric about C (and D). The perceived elevation is thus neither consistent with the 3-D nor with the 2-D relationships, but influenced by both.

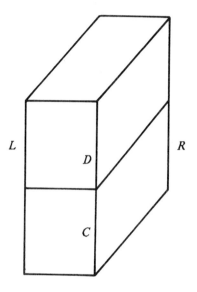

Figure 2.22 Segments L and R in this figure are exactly symmetric about C and D. According to the uninterpreted distance hypothesis C-R and C-L should have the same CS.

The perceived distance (i.e. the distance in the image plane as judged by observers) is also biased by the 3-D interpretation, so that the perceived separations (e.g. of D-L vs. D-R) will be somewhere between the pure 2-D and the interpreted 3-D distances. One can thus distinguish between three kinds of distances. One is the 2-D uninterpreted separation. The second is the 3-D separation implied by the spatial interpretation of the scene.   The third is the perceived distance, influenced by both the 2-D and the 3-D distances (c.f. [Attneave & Frost, 1969] and the "phenomenal separation" in [Attneave & Block, 1973]).   In the last two cases the correspondence will be said to depend on the *interpreted* distance, whereas in the first case it depends on the *uninterpreted* distance.   The problem considered in this section is which of the three distances is relevant to the correspondence process.

There are several reasons for examining this problem in detail.   The main reason is that it is an important aspect of the correspondence problem, and a general one that should be clarified before turning to the details.   The effect of the distance in the matching process is a major one, and consequently it becomes pertinent to disambiguate the term "distance".   The problem is also directly relevant to the *level* at which the correspondence is carried out.   If the construction of a spatial model of the scene precedes the correspondence process, the preference for matching nearest neighbors might be based on the 3-D distances in the model.   On the other hand, from the preceding sections it should be expected that the correspondence is established independently of the 3-D interpretation, and hence that the uninterpreted distance should govern the matching process.   This last expectation seems to run contrary to experimental evidence reported in the psychological literature.   Studies by Corbin [1942] and by Attneave and Block [1973] were interpreted as supporting the view that interpreted distance underlies (or at least strongly influences) the correspondence process.   However, all previous studies were based on the paradigm of *smoothness judgments* whose applicability to the correspondence problem is, as we have already mentioned, dubious.   A secondary goal of this section is, therefore, to critically examine the relations between smoothness of motion and correspondence strength.

The conclusions in this section are based on the experiments reported in [Ullman, 1978a].   In the experiments, direct comparisons of correspondence strength were used to determine the kind of distance governing the correspondence

process. Various figures were constructed, showing a line
segment in alternation with two other segments, one to its left,
the second to its right. In some of the displays the lines were
embedded in configurations having clear 3-D interpretations.
The perceived motion was then analyzed to test the different
distance hypotheses. In one example, segment D in Figure 2.22
was tested in competing motion with segments L and R. Due to
the 3-D interpretation of the figure, the distances of D to L and
D to R appear markedly different. If an internal 3-D model of
the figure is indeed constructed prior to the matching operation,
the D-L motion should prevail since this distance will be smaller
in the model than the D-R distance. The prediction based on
the interpreted distance hypotheses is therefore that when D is
presented in apparent motion with both L and R, the motion
towards L will be judged by observers as stronger, by an amount
that had been estimated in a related experiment. Since the D-L
and D-R distances are identical in the image plane, the
uninterpreted distance hypothesis predicts that the two competing
motions will be of equal likelihood. When the lines where
actually tested in motion, the two competing motions occured
with equal likelihood. The results of this, as well as a number
of other experiments, lead to the conclusion that it is the
uninterpreted distance that governs the correspondence process.

These results were obtained using the competing motion
technique that compares CS directly. As mentioned above,
different results were obtained in similar experiments where
smoothness of motion criteria were employed. It is of interest,
therefore, to examine these differences more closely.

2.5.2 Correspondence Strength and Smoothness of Motion

The ISI required for optimal apparent motion to occur depends
on the spatial separation between the stimuli: this was originally
stated as Korte's third law [Korte, 1915]. Is the relevant
separation in this case the 2-D or the perceptual distance?
Corbin [1942] and Attneave and Block [1973] addressed this

question experimentally. They found that smoothness (or optimality) of motion is determined predominantly, perhaps even solely, by perceptual distance. Kolers [1972, Chapters 4 and 5] as well as earlier researchers (e.g., Brown and Voth [1937]) examined problems pertaining to the CS using smoothness of motion as a criterion for the CS. But the assumption that smoothness of motion measures correspondence strength is inconsistent with the results mentioned above. Namely, the following three claims are inconsistent:

1. Smoothness of motion depends on perceptual distance.
2. The CS depends on 2-D distance.
3. Smoothness of motion is a measure of the CS.

Now the first two claims have been tested experimentally, but the third never was. It therefore became desirable at this point to test the third claim directly. A test of this last claim can be carried out in the following way. First, lines C and L, with L parallel to C and lying to its left, are shown in alternation, and the intervals needed for optimal motion to occur are measured. A time interval $[t_1, t_2]$ is thereby determined, such that if the ISI satisfies the requirement $t_1 < ISI < t_2$, then C and L are seen in smooth motion. Next, the same procedure is repeated for a second pair of lines, C and R, where R lies to the right of C, and the C-R distance is larger than the distance C-L. (L does not participate in this display.) A new range of intervals $[T_1, T_2]$ is thereby obtained for the C-L pair. Finally, C is shown in alternation with *both* L and R, using an interval which satisfies: $T_1, t_2 < ISI < T_2$. This ISI falls within the smoothness range for the C to R motion, but not for the motion between C and L. What percept should arise? According to assumption 3 above, the motion should be predominantly between C and R.

Such an experiment has been carried out, and is reported in [Ullman, 1978a]. Intervals of smooth motion were obtained for pairs of vertical lines in isolation (i.e. without any background context). The distance between C and L was 0.7 degrees of visual angle, while C and R were 4.5 degrees apart.

The mean value for t_2, the upper smoothness limit for the closer lines was 115.4 msec. (S.D. = 26.2) and for T_2 172.7 (S.D. = 34). These averages, however, were not used in the experiment. Instead, optimal motion ranges were established for each subject individually, and an ISI satisfying the above requirements was then computed. Of 12 observers that participated in the experiment, 10 reported a motion between C and L only, one reported a strong preference to the left, and one a weak preference to the left.

Conclusion: the inconsistency raised in this section is resolved by rejecting the third proposition. Smoothness of motion *cannot* serve as an indication for the correspondence strength.

2.5.3 General Conclusions

Two main results follow from the above experiments, one relating to the nature of the correspondence problem, the other to the relation between smoothness of motion and the correspondence strength. The finding that smoothness is not a faithful measure of the CS warns against concentration on the study of apparent motion through "optimality of motion" judgments. At least as far as the correspondence problem is concerned, considerations based on optimality of motion might be misleading, and thus the large number of studies based on smoothness of motion cannot be accepted as applicable to the problem at hand.

By using a competing motion technique which compares CS directly, it has been concluded that the two-dimensional separation governs the CS. Two distinctions are worth mentioning in the context of this finding. First, 2-D distance should not necessarily be identified with retinal separation. That the two might indeed be different was demonstrated by Rock and Ebenholtz [1962]. Second, depth obtained from disparity data was excluded from the experiments, since disparity can be obtained at a low level, independent of the scene interpretation, as had been demonstrated by Julesz [1971]. The possible effect of stereo information on the CS remains to be clarified in further studies.

2.5.4 Semantic Interpretation

The effect of semantic interpretation on the correspondence
established between moving objects has been examined is several
studies. Jones & Bruner [1954], for example, compared the
perceived motion between stick-men figures to the motion of
nonsense figures. However, since the study was based on
smoothness comparisons, it cannot be accepted as relevant to the
correspondence problem.

A study that examined the effects of semantic interpretation using a competing motion technique rather than
smoothness judgments was carried out by Toch and Ittelon
[1956]. They claimed to have found an effect of semantic interpretation on the matching process. Their experiment consisted
of two displays. One display tested a downwards pointing bomb-
figure in competing motion with two other bombs, one above
and one below it. The second display tested an upwards
pointing airplane-figure with airplanes above and below it. The
claim was that for the bomb the downward motion was somewhat
preferred, while for the airplane it was the upward motion, as
might be expected from the semantic content of the scene.

There are, however, reasons for not accepting the above
result as indicative of the CS. A major reason is the lack of
monitoring of eye movements. The above results might be
expected if the subject's eyes wander in accordance with the
expected motion (c.f. the "block train" in Section 1.3). I have
experimented with displays of arrows pointing in various
directions, and found no effect of semantic interpretation as long
as the subject fixates at the center of the display. Some of the
studies by Navon [1976] that employed competing motion techniques are also relevant to the problem of semantic interpretation
and motion correspondence. Although Navon was interested in
figural similarity, some of his displays also contrasted
semantically identical versus dissimilar elements (e.g. English

letters) in competing motion. The reported results show no effect of semantic similarity on the pairings, thus supporting the view that motion correspondence is independent of semantic interpretation. It seems, in conclusion, that the only demonstrable effect of semantic interpretation on the correspondence process is indirect, via eye motions. If the eyes remain stationary, semantic interpretation, like 3-D interpretation, exerts no influence on the correspondence strengths.

The current findings support the view that the correspondence process is a low level operation which precedes, or is independent of, the interpretation of the scene. Such a low level operation can provide an explanation for the perceptual identity of objects in motion or change. The human visual system is capable of correctly identifying different views of a moving object as representing the same physical entity. Objects in change can also retain their identity: a frog in an animated movie can change into a prince before our very eyes without ever losing its identity. It might be conjectured that the identity is retained since the correspondence process, operating at a low level, declares the views as corresponding, i.e. as different representations of the same entity, regardless of the subsequent 3-D and semantic interpretations.

A low-level, autonomous correspondence process has also the potential of being utilized by other perceptually related processes. In the next section such a possibility is discussed.

2.6 A Possible Application to Object Concept Incipiency

This section raises the possibility that the correspondence process might play an important role in the early stages of concept formation. The goal is not to make a well supported conjecture, since sufficient data are as yet unavailable. Rather, it is to suggest that the availability of an autonomous correspondence process might have implications pertaining to the perception and conceptualization of objects. I wish to point to a possible scheme which has been largely overlooked, probably because the correspondence process has not usually been conceived of as a primitive, autonomous process. Though speculative, this section has specific implications that may possibly be studied experimentally.

One of the most fundamental aspects of cognitive growth in infancy is the formation of object concepts [Bower, 1966, 1971, 1974; Gibson, 1969; Day & McKenzie, 1973; Cohen & Salapatek, 1975]. That is, the process by which an infant, devoid of any acquaintance with material objects, develops into a infant who evidently possesses knowledge about objects and their properties.

The understanding of this process poses two main problems. First, what is the time course of its development, namely, what do infants at differents ages know about material objects. Second, how is this knowledge derived by the child on the basis of his sensory exposure to the environment.

The formation of an object concept has many facets, one of which is the ability to link together different views that belong to a single object. Two alternative views arise when trying to explain this linking ability. The linkage might be based on some rudimentary concept formation, or the relation might be reversed, with the emergence of object concepts being contingent upon the linking ability. According to the first view, the infant might first come to some sort of understanding that a certain view $V1$ with which he is presented represents some object $O1$, and a different view $V2$ represents an object $O2$. The two views $V1$ and $V2$ are linked together only when the infant comes to realize, on a tactile basis perhaps, that $O1$ and $O2$ are one and the same object. In this approach the linking of the views is founded upon the existence of some rudimentary object concept, and therefore runs the risk of circularity in explaining the origin of object concepts using object concepts. Alternatively, it might be the case that $V1$ and $V2$ are spontaneously linked together into a group, which in turn serves as the basis for the incipient object concept. Such an approach to the concept formation problem requires that two basic operations be performed by the child. The first is the spontaneous linkage of different views that belong to a single object into one group, and the second is the ability to attach properties to the group as a whole. Let me clarify this by way of an example.

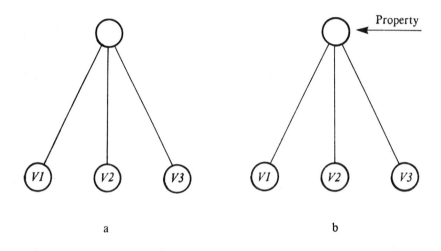

Figure 2.23   Different views are linked together to a super-ordinate node (2.23a). Properties are attached to the super-ordinate node and thereby to all the views at once (2.23b).

Suppose that when an infant sees different views of a given object, a bottle, say, he can group them together in a manner that can be graphically described as linking them all to a super-ordinate entity in his representation of the world (Figure 2.23a). The ability to attach properties to the group as a whole can be met by attaching them to the new super-ordinate "node", even when the properties are learned in the context of a particular view or set of views, as diagrammed in Figure 2.23b.

To appreciate the implication of the two operations consider the following scenario. An infant is given an empty bottle with which to play, and is thereby exposed to different views thereof. When he cries for food, he is given the bottle, filled with food this time, but in such a way that only some of the possible bottle-views are visible when the bottle makes its way to the infant's mouth. After some time, the infant will probably learn to associate the food expectation with the bottle view. If he possesses the two operations listed above, the food expectation will be associated not with some of the bottle views but with the super-ordinate node, and hence with *all the views at once*. One view of the bottle will elicit the same response in the hungry child as any other one, although the food had been associated in the past with only a subset of the bottle views. Such a child can be said to have a rudimentary concept of the bottle. His behavior can be described as understanding to a degree that the food-giving property belongs to the bottle-object rather than to particular views of it.

There is, therefore, an advantage to the proposal that the linkage of appearances to one another precedes, rather than follows, the formation of a rudimentary object concept. If some distinction between objects and their appearances were a prerequisite for linking together the different views of an object, then it remains to be explained what constitutes this distinction and how it comes about. But if the process of grouping appearances is independent of any prior knowledge of objects, it helps to break the circularity involved in basing the emergence of object concepts on the existence of some kind of rudimentary object concepts. It also becomes unnecessary to assume that the young infant understand what constitutes an external object in any deep sense. The two basic processes (linking views and attaching properties) can actually *serve* in their very operation as a first stage in the understanding of what an object is.

The possible scheme for object concept formation outlined above requires that different views of a given object, dissimilar as they might be, are linked to each other but not to the views of other objects. But how can the different views of an object be singled out without any knowledge of what the object is? Several possible candidates have been proposed in the past for selecting and linking views together, although not always explicitly considered for this task. The main candidates are associations, Piaget's multi-modal experience, and Bower's "same place" notion.

The associationists from Locke to J.S. Mill held that collections of sensory impressions are grouped together into clusters on the basis of such criteria as simultaneity, spatial proximity and similarity. In Piaget's view [Piaget, 1954] the acquisition of object concept depends on inter-modal learning, in particular on the combination of visual and tactile explorations. Thus, the grasping sense can provide the information that a certain object is one and the same when it changes its appearance during manipulation. Bower [1971] advanced the notion that the identity of an object is established primarily on the basis of its location. If an object changes its appearance but remains at the same location its different views will be perceived as being, at least in some sense, the same thing.

I will not digress here to examine the above hypotheses, but rather advance a new possibility which might be particularly suitable for the task. Two views can be linked together if they *stand in a correspondence relation*, i.e., if one of them transforms through motion into the other.

I have argued in the preceding sections that the correspondence is a low-level autonomous process, which can operate independently of familiarity with and recognition of objects. Everyday experience illustrates the success of the correspondence process. Its proficiency is manifested by the fact that objects, including moving ones, do not lose their perceptual identity and do not merge into other objects. It is therefore expected that whenever two views are matched by the correspondence process on the basis of their affinities and certain spatio-temporal relationships, they do indeed represent the same object. Consequently, they can be safely linked together to form the required basis for the evolving object concept.

The hypothesis advanced above can be examined experimentally. For example, an infant can be presented with a view *V1* of some object, which transforms through smooth motion into a different view *V2*. The infant is then trained to associate a certain property with *V1* and the transfer of the learning to *V2* is examined. The motion-based transfer can be compared with the effect produced by, for instance, *V1* and *V2* being in close temporal succession but not in perceptually smooth motion. The prediction from the motion-based hypothesis is that the transfer will be markedly enhanced in the change-through-motion case.

The foregoing section raises the following view of the relation between the concept of an object and the understanding of objects in motion. Rather than beginning with the concept of a static object and the different views thereof, and then using the emerging structure to appreciate objects in motion, the reverse situation might exist. The linkage of views based on the correspondence through motion occurs first, and thereby a representational structure is set up, that serves as a basis for the understanding of what an object is.

CHAPTER 3

THE MINIMAL MAPPING THEORY
OF MOTION CORRESPONDENCE

3.1 Introduction

In this chapter the correspondence problem will be approached from a computational point of view, addressing the question of how motion correspondence might be successfully established. The objective here is to devise a workable correspondence scheme that can actually solve the matching problem, and account for the relevant data concerning the correspondence established by the human visual system.

The range of possible correspondence strategies to be considered is determined, to a large degree, by the level at which the matching process is performed. That is, the strategy depends upon the elements that would be matched, e.g., whether they are high-level constructs such as perceived objects [c.f. Warren, 1977; Ullman, 1977b], or low-level units, such as points, blobs, edge fragments, line segments, and certain groups thereof. Chapters 1 and 2 presented arguments and evidence in support of the latter view. For the correspondence process, the input image at any given time may thus be viewed simply as a collection of elementary tokens, and the theory of matching these tokens would provide an adequate basis for the theory of motion correspondence in general.

We shall start by considering the correspondence problem in a simplified version, in which two "frames" are presented in succession, resulting in apparent motion. We shall further assume that each frame consists only of isolated dots of equal intensity. Subsequently, the analysis will be extended to other types of elements, and to continuous motion.

In our search for a plausible correspondence procedure, we shall use guidelines from "above" and constraints from "below". The guidelines from "above" are properties of physical motion which can be used to solve the correspondence problem. The constraints from "below" are those imposed by computational considerations in general, and by the requirement that the computation be feasible in a biological system in particular.

3.2 The Optimal (Independent) Correspondence Strategy

Given the two frames, the problem we face is how to establish a correspondence between their elements. Assuming there are n elements in each frame, there are $n!$ different one-to-one mappings between them. Hence we face a problem of ambiguity common to various aspects of visual analysis, namely, that the visual input admits more than a single interpretation. In light of such an ambiguity, no method is immune to misinterpretation. However, if some properties of the visible environment render some interpretations more likely than others, it becomes possible to select the most likely solution, thus maximizing the probability of interpreting the input correctly. We shall therefore seek a correspondence scheme that will maximize the probability of yielding a correct interpretation [3.1].

The selection of the most plausible correspondence requires the utilization of information concerning the plausibility of different matches. Such additional information can belong to one of two categories: general or particular. In using particular information, one brings to bear knowledge applicable to a specific situation, for example, the assumption that the black blob on the desk in one's office is a telephone. Examples of general knowledge are the rigidity constraint in the interpretation of structure from motion (introduced in Chapter 4) which is based on properties of rigid objects in general, or the two constraints governing the matching process in stereopsis [Marr and Poggio, 1976]. If motion correspondence is established at a low level, then information of the general kind should be applied. In the following section, properties of moving elements in general will be used to guide the matching process.

The independence hypothesis

The selection of the most likely correspondence requires a method for comparing the likelihood of different possible matches. To determine the likelihood of a match, it is necessary to know what dependencies are assumed to hold between the motions of individual elements. For example: if X and Y are neighboring elements and X moves to the right, is Y more likely to move to the right than to the left? Since our prime objective is the investigation of human motion perception, we want our underlying assumptions to be consistent with the correspondence process as performed by the human visual system. When the human correspondence process is examined using simple displays containing a small number of elements, no such biases are apparent. The configuration in Figure 3.1 demonstrates this lack of bias. Points $X1$ and $X2$ are presented in apparent motion with $Y1$, $Y2$, and $Y3$. (In all the figures unfilled circles will denote the first presentation, and crosses the second. A cross inside an unfilled circle means that this element participated in both the first and second frame.) If only $X1$, $Y1$ and $Y2$ are presented, $X1$ moves to the right or to the left with equal probability. It will usually split and move in both directions at once. When $X2$ and $Y3$ are presented as well, $X2$ is seen to move to the right and match $Y3$. Will this motion increase the likelihood of seeing $X1$ as moving to the right to match $Y2$? The answer is that no such preference is apparent, provided that fixation is maintained at the center.

In Chapter 2 we have seen that competition interactions were necessary to account for the matching process, but there was no need for "positive" interactions between matches of similar directions. We shall generalize from these observations and accept the hypothesis that the elements are treated as moving independently of each other [3.2]. We shall next develop the optimal correspondence strategy, given this independence hypothesis. It will subsequently be shown that the emerging

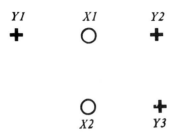

Figure 3.1 Lack of "positive interactions" between matches.

method remains optimal under conditions that would violate the independence hypothesis, and that the incorporation of dependencies between directions would be redundant.

The maximum likelihood correspondence

Suppose that n elements are moving in space independently of each other, at various speeds, and in different directions. Two "snapshots" of the moving elements are taken, and a match is to be established between the "input elements" in the first image and the "output elements" in the second. Let $p(v)$ denote the probability distribution of the velocity of the elements in the image plane. That is to say, if a moving element is selected at random, the probability that its velocity v in the image plane lies between values a and b is:

$$\int_a^b p(v)\, dv \tag{1}$$

Given the independence hypothesis, the probability of having a collection of n elements, with the ith element $(1 \leq i \leq n)$ covering a distance d_i in time interval t, is determined by the product:

$$\prod_i p(v_i) \qquad\qquad (2)$$

where $v_i = d_i/t$.   The most likely match will therefore be found by maximizing (2) over all the legal matches between the two frames (the one-to-one mappings in this case).   In what follows it will be convenient to transform the product in (2) into a sum. Since the logarithmic function is monotonic, and all the $p(v_i)$ are positive, the most likely match can equivalently be found by the solution to:

$$\min \Sigma\, q(v_i) \qquad\qquad (3)$$

where the minimum is taken over all the legal matches, and $q(v)$ = -log $p(v)$.   If $0 \le p(v) \le 1$, then $q(v)$ will be a non-negative function.

(Comment: the index of summation, i in this case, will be omitted throughout the remainder of this chapter whenever it is unambiguous.)   If $q(v)$ is thought of as a "cost" function, then the optimal mapping minimizes the total cost over all the legal matches.

Mappings which are not one-to-one

If the number of input elements does not equal the number of output elements, the mapping between them cannot be one-to-one.   The simplest example of this situation is the split motion configuration (see Figure 2.3) where X is presented in apparent motion with both $Y1$ and $Y2$. The one-to-one condition must be violated in this case.   This can occur in one of two ways.   Either X is mapped to a single element, leaving the other without a "partner", or, it can split and match both $Y1$ and $Y2$. (If $Y1$ and $Y2$ precede X, then the two elements might both match X, a situation we called *fusion*).   Perceptually, the split or fusion possibility is usually preferred over the "no match" situation (unless one of the distances is much larger than the other).   We shall therefore require that legal matches be *covers*. A cover is defined as a match in which every input element is paired with at least one output element, and every output element is paired with at least one input element.   How should the optimal match be determined in these non one-to-one cases?

The independence hypothesis as formulated above does not directly apply to situations in which elements split and fuse. For the sake of simplicity, we shall extend the independence hypothesis to include covers as well. Some further modifications of the optimal mapping will be introduced later, after a method for computing optimal matches has been presented. For the present, the optimal match will be determined, as before, by minimizing the cost $\Sigma\ q(v_i)$ over all the legal matches. The only modification is that the set of legal matches is extended to include all covers. In graph-theoretic terms the optimal match defined in this way is called the "minimum weighted cover of a bipartite graph". (In a bipartite graph the set of vertices V satisfies $V = V_1 \cup V_2$, where $V_1 \cap V_2 = \emptyset$, and each arc connects a vertex in V_1 to a vertex in V_2.) For brevity, we shall use the term *minimal mapping* to denote the *match that minimizes* Σq_i *over the covers of the graph of possible pairings.*

We turn next to examine the plausibility of the minimal mapping, and to compare it with the human correspondence process. In Chapter 2 we have seen that the eventual correspondence is derived from the original affinities via local interactions. The next section provides theoretical reasons for why such a scheme might be necessary. We then face an essential problem, namely whether the minimal mapping is compatible with the scheme based on affinities and local interactions. Sections 4 and 5 provide a positive answer to this question. They establish the local nature of the correspondence problem, and lead to a method for computing the minimal mapping from the underlying affinities via simple, local interactions.

3.3 Computational Feasibility

The minimal mapping solution is obviously computable, for instance, by enumeration: the sum $\Sigma\ q(v_i)$ can be computed for all the legal matches, and a minimum can then be selected. Due to its inefficiency, however, such an algorithm would be unreasonable. Is there a feasible method of computing the minimal mapping? The feasibility of a computation depends, to a large extent, on properties of the processor which executes it, and therefore the question cannot be settled without making some assumption about the way the computation is carried out. Since the correspondence computation is performed by the human visual system, we wish our notion of computational feasibilty to include the requirements for "biological feasibility". We shall then be able to inquire whether the minimal mapping computation can reasonably be expected to be incorporated in the human visual system. Without committing ourselves to a particular model, we shall make three general assumptions about the way in which the correspondence process is achieved by the human visual system. We shall then investigate whether the computation of the minimal mapping is feasible, given these assumptions. The three assumptions are parallelism, simplicity, and locality.

Parallelism: Since the correspondence process operates on low-level elements, and there might be a large number of them in a given image, the pairing of corresponding elements is assumed to be accomplished, to a large extent, in parallel.

Locality: If the number of "processors" performing the correspondence computation is large, it becomes infeasible to connect each of them to all of the others. It will therefore be assumed that there are only local connections between the processors, e.g., each processor is only connected to its r nearest neighboring processors [3.3]. The number r will be called the "radius of the computation".

Simplicity: If there is a large number of processors, it seems reasonable to assume that each of the individual processors is a rather simple computing device. We shall not attempt here to define simplicity precisely, however note that simplicity refers to the individual processors, not to the entire process.

We shall combine the above assumptions in the notion of

a *simple network*, which stands for a locally connected network of simple processors. In the ideal case, all the processors are identical, and each one is connected to *r* of its neighbors. In the correspondence computation, processors are "assigned" to the elements in the image, and their task is to find (in parallel) the matches for the elements.

We have listed some theoretical reasons for assuming that motion correspondence is carried out by a simple network. Chapter 2 provided evidence in support of the view that the correspondence process employed by the human visual system is indeed simple and local.

General issues such as computability, efficiency and locality in simple networks of this kind are as yet little understood. Rather then addressing them directly, we shall restrict our discussion to their relationship with the correspondence process. Since the minimal mapping has been advanced as an optimal matching strategy, and simple networks as a plausible computational model, the main problem addressed in the next section will be: *can the minimal mapping method be computed by a simple network?* (It should be noted that such simple networks are not, in general, equivalent to a universal computing machine [3.4].)

The prospects of performing the minimal mapping computation with a simple network might seem dubious, due to the discrete, combinatorial nature of the problem. However, we shall see that the minimal mapping correspondence can be computed if the definition of legal matches is changed somewhat. Instead of the set of all covers, we consider a subset of local covers. For each element there are N neighbors which are the *initial candidates* for a legal match [3.5]. A legal match is one in which each element is paired with (at least) one of its initial candidates. Of these legal matches, the one that minimizes $\Sigma q(v_i)$ is sought. We shall verify in the following section that in this formulation the optimal match is computable by a simple local process. We shall also determine the radius of the computation, that is, to how many neighbors each processor must connect in order to make the minimal mapping computation possible. As we shall see, it is sufficient that each processor be connected only to its initial candidates (i.e., $r = N$, where r is the radius of the computation, and N the number of initial candidates). This is by no means obvious. Although each element is paired with one of its initial candidates, owing to the global requirements for consistency and optimality (i.e. that the resulting mapping will be a minimum cost cover) the match assigned to a given element might depend on the matching of elements far beyond its initial candidates.

3.4 Computing the Minimal Mapping by a Simple Network

In this and the following section, I shall examine the problem of computing the minimal mapping by a simple, local network. The treatment is formal in nature, and for the convenience of those who might wish to avoid the mathematical analysis, the main results are summarized at the beginning of Sections 3.4 and 3.5.

The main-result established in these sections is that the minimal mapping, and thus the most likely correspondence, can be computed from the underlying affinities via simple local interactions. The minimal mapping is thus compatible in this respect with the scheme described in Chapter 2. The affinities of Chapter 2 are inversely related to the cost q (e.g., the affinity might be equal to C - q, where C is a sufficiently large constant), so that minimizing the cost q is equivalent to maximizing the affinities. According to this view, the human correspondence process leads to a maximization of the total affinity, and thereby establishes the most likely match. A method by which a simple network can compute the minimal mapping is presented in Section 3.4.

The development of the method involves two stages:
  1. Reformulating the computation of the minimal mapping as a Linear Programming (LP) problem. A theorem from Integer

Programming (IP) ensures the equivalence of the original problem and the LP formulation. This stage transforms the matching problem from the discrete form of pairing elements to a continuous optimization problem.

2. Employing a method devised by Arrow, Hurwicz and Uzawa [1958] to solve the resulting LP problem by a simple, local, process.

Reformulating the minimal mapping as an LP problem

Linear Programming (LP) is the study of optimizing linear functions subject to linear constraints. In vector notation, an LP problem is:

Minimize $\underline{c}*\underline{x}$ (4)

Subject to: $A\underline{x} \geq \underline{b}$

$\underline{x} \geq 0$

Where $A = (a_{ij})$ is an m*n matrix, $\underline{x}$ and $\underline{c}$ are n-dimensional vectors, and $\underline{b}$ an m-dimensional vector. In a more explicit form, we wish to find a vector $\underline{x} = (x_1, x_2, ..., x_n)$ that will minimize $\sum_i c_i x_i$ subject to m constraints on the x_i's. The jth constraint is: $\sum_k a_{jk} x_k \geq b_j$, and $x_i \geq 0$ for $i = 1,...,n$.

To recast the minimal mapping problem in terms of LP we shall introduce the variables x_{ij}, $1 \leq i \leq n$ (if there are n input elements) $1 \leq j \leq m$ (if there are m output elements). If an input element i is paired with an output element j, then $x_{ij} = 1$, otherwise $x_{ij} = 0$. In a cover, $\sum_j x_{ij} \geq 1$ for all i, and $\sum_i x_{ij} \geq 1$ for all j. We shall therefore formulate the following LP problem:

Minimize $\sum x_{ij} q_{ij}$ (5)

Subject to: $\sum_j x_{ij} \geq 1$ for $1 \leq i \leq n$

$\sum_i x_{ij} \geq 1$ for $1 \leq j \leq m$

$x_{ij} \geq 0$ for $1 \leq i \leq n$, $1 \leq j \leq m$

Comments: 1) The total number of variables x_{ij} is nN, since there are n input elements, each having N output neighbors.

2) q_{ij} is the cost of the link between input element i and output element j.

Is this LP problem equivalent to the original minimal mapping problem? It would be, if we add the restriction that each x_{ij} can assume binary values only (i.e. $x_{ij} = 1$ or $x_{ij} = 0$). The additional restriction cannot be expressed in the LP formalism, but fortunately it is redundant. A theorem from Integer Programming states that there exists an optimal solution to the above LP problem in which all the x_{ij} are *integers* [Garfinkel & Nemhauser; 1972]. (Note that the constraints matrix is unimodular.) It is straightforward to verify that the integer condition implies that the only possible values for the x_{ij} in the optimal solution are 0 or 1. Consequently, assuming that the optimal solution is unique, any algorithm that solves the LP problem is also guaranteed to solve the original minimal mapping problem. In the rare cases where the optimal solution is not unique, there are at least two different optimal integral solutions, as well as non-integral solutions. For the present, we shall assume that the optimal solution is unique. The non-unique case is examined in Section 3.6.

We shall next describe a method of solving the LP problem which can be carried out by a simple network.

Computing the minimal mapping in a simple network

A method of optimizing functions in which the computation is distributed between simple, locally connected processors, was introduced by Arrow *et al* [1958]. This method is based on a theorem by Kuhn and Tucker [1951] which states the equivalence between optimal solutions to the constrained problem, and saddle points of the associated Lagrangian.

Consider the problem of maximizing a function $f(x)$ subject to m constraints $g_i(x) \geq 0$, $i = 1,...,m$. The *Lagrangian* associated with the problem is defined as:

$$L(x,u) = f(x) + \Sigma \, u_i g_i \qquad (6)$$

where x is an n-dimensional and u an m-dimensional vector.

A non-negative saddle point of the above Lagrangian is a non-negative point (x',u') satisfying:

$$L(x,u') \leq L(x',u') \leq L(x',u) \qquad \text{for every } x \geq 0, u \geq 0 \quad (7)$$

Theorem: (Kuhn and Tucker) If (i) $f(x)$ and $g_i(x)$ are concave, and (ii) there exists a vector $x_0 \geq 0$ such that $g_i(x_0) > 0$ ($1 \leq i \leq m$), then a vector x' is a solution to the maximization problem if and only if there exists a vector u' such that (x',u') is a saddle point of the associated Lagrangian.

(In the above formulation the conditions are slightly different from those in the original Kuhn-Tucker theorem. For a proof, see Arrow, Hurwicz and Uzawa, Chapter 3.) Note that the LP formulation of the correspondence problem satisfies the conditions of the Kuhn-Tucker theorem; $f(x)$ and $g_i(x)$ are linear, and for x_0 one can consider, for example, the vector with $x_{ij} = 2$ for all i, j.

The Lagrangian gradient method

The Kuhn-Tucker theorem, which is an extension of the classical Lagrange Multipliers theory, transforms the problem of optimizing a constrained function to the problem of determining a saddle-point of the associated Lagrangian. Arrow *et al* [1958] investigated the possibility of computing saddle points using gradient methods. A gradient method searches for a saddle-point of $L(x,u)$ by moving in the direction of the local gradients ("uphill" in x, "downhill" in u), without violating the non-negativity condition on the variables. This search is defined in terms of the Arrow-Hurwicz differential equations [*ibid*, p. 118]:

$$\dot{x}(t) = 0 \text{ if } x_i = 0 \text{ and } Lx_i < 0 \tag{8}$$

$$\dot{x}(t) = Lx_i \text{ otherwise}$$

$$\dot{u}(t) = 0 \text{ if } u_i = 0 \text{ and } Lu_i > 0$$

$$\dot{u}(t) = -Lu_i \text{ otherwise}$$

where Lx_i is the partial derivative of the Lagrangian with respect to x_i, and Lu_i with respect to u_i. An approximation to the Arrow-Hurwicz equation can be defined by the following iterations:

$$x_i^{n+1} = \max [0, x_i^n + \rho \, Lx_i] \qquad (9)$$
$$u_i^{n+1} = \max [0, u_i^n - \rho \, Lu_i]$$

where ρ is a selected step size. If L in the formulae is the Lagrangian as defined in the Kuhn-Tucker theorem, the method is called the "naive" Lagrangian method. The main point to notice is that the naive gradient computation of the minimal mapping problem is simple and local. The reason for the locality is that the values of Lx_i and Lu_i are given in terms of the values of x and u in the ith processor and its N immediate neighbors only. More specifically, the Lagrangian is:

$$L(x,u) = -\Sigma \, q_{ij}x_{ij} + \Sigma_i u_i(\Sigma_j x_{ij} - 1) + \Sigma_j v_j(\Sigma_i x_{ij} - 1) \quad (10)$$

The u_i and v_j are all Lagrange multipliers. The u_i are associated with the input elements and the v_j with the output elements. If there are n input and m output elements then $i = 1,...,n$ and $j = 1,...,m$. The derivatives take the simple form:

$$Lx_{ij} = u_i + v_j - q_{ij}$$
$$Lu_i = \Sigma_i x_{ij} - 1$$
$$Lv_j = \Sigma_j x_{ij} - 1$$

Since the derivatives are local, the processes defined by (8) and (9) are local. Note that in order to compute the minimal mapping by this method, each processor must compute only a very simple function of its neighbors. Figure 3.2 depicts a portion of the network that computes the above correspondence process. The input elements are denoted by circles, the output elements by squares. The processor u_i is associated with the ith input element, the processor v_j with the jth output element, and the processor x_{ij} with the link between the ith input element and the jth output element. Each processor in this network computes

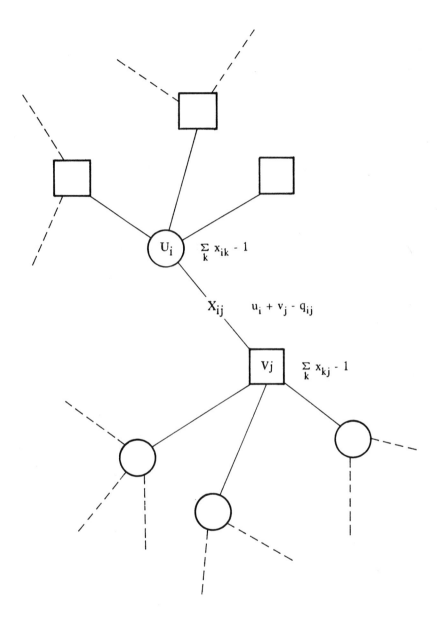

Figure 3.2 A portion of the simple network that performs the minimal mapping computation. Next to the processors, the quantities they have to compute are indicated.

a simple function of its immediate neighbors. To go from their current state to the subsequent state, the processors must compute the following quantities (the Lagrangian's derivatives):

x_{ij} computes $u_i + v_j - q_{ij}$

u_i computes $\sum_k x_{ik} - 1$, where the sum is taken over the arcs radiating from u_i.

v_j computes $\sum_k x_{kj} - 1$, where the sum is taken over the arcs leading into v_j.

Convergence

The Arrow-Hurwicz method is said to converge to a solution if $(x(t), u(t))$ approaches a saddle point of $L(x,u)$ as $t \to \infty$. The naive gradient method as defined above is not guaranteed to converge to a solution. If $L(x,u)$ is linear in both x and u, the solution might go instead into a limit-cycle [Arrow et al, 1958; Chapter 6]. However, there are possible ways of improving this behavior. For example, the process might exploit the fact that the ultimate value of each x_{ij} is constrained to be either 0 or 1 by introducing a threshold operation: a link whose x_{ij} value exceeds a certain threshold will become a part of the cover, while a link whose x_{ij} falls below a certain threshold will be eliminated. Such an operation might also serve the purpose of speeding up the process, since the convergence of (9) is usually slow [3.6].

There are also general methods for modifying the naive Lagrangian method in a way that will ensure the global convergence of the Arrow-Hurwicz equations to a saddle-point (of both the modified and the original Lagrangian), and hence to an optimal solution. For example, the modified Lagrangian LM can be defined as [Arrow et al, 1958; p. 137]:

$$LM(x,u) = f(x) + \sum u_i \, \psi_i[g_i(x)] \qquad (11)$$

where the functions ψ_i are strictly increasing, strictly concave analytic functions with $\psi_i(0) = 0$. (An example of such a function is $\psi(z) = 1 - e^{-rz}$ for $r > 0$.) When the continuous process in (8) is applied to the modified Lagrangian, convergence is guaranteed for any concave f and g, including the linear case. Note that the gradient method applied to the modified Lagrangian still yields a local computation, similar to the naive gradient case (albeit not quite as simple).

If the iterative procedure in (9) is applied to this modified Lagrangian, the iteration will usually converge to a solution as well [3.7]. Furthermore, it is also possible to modify the original Lagrangian in such a way as to guarantee the global convergence of the iterative procedure to a solution, provided that the step-size ρ is sufficiently small, while maintaining the locality property of the procedure. As before, the gradients LMx and LMu computed for the ith component will depend only on the ith processor and its N immediate neighbors.

Conclusions

The minimal mapping, which under the independence assumption is also the optimal match, can be determined by a simple, local computation. One can envision a network of simple processing elements which accepts two "snapshots" of elements in motion, and finds the most likely correspondence between them via local interactions. The above method can be applied to other problems of constrained optimization computed by local processes, [Ullman, 1978c]. It should be noted that the above scheme used the simplification that a match has two states; it is either present ($x_{ij} = 1$) or absent ($x_{ij} = 0$). There was no attempt to associate "strength" with the match, as was done in Chapter 2. Strength can enter the scheme in various ways. For example, although x_{ij} converges to 0 or 1 exclusively, until it converges it might assume intermediate values between 0 and 1, which can be used to indicate the strength of the match.

3.5 Preference for One-to-one Mappings

The minimal mapping method as presented above does not "penalize" matches for deviating from the one-to-one mapping. Such a simplification is unsatisfactory on both theoretical and empirical grounds.

On the theoretical side, splits and fusions of elements in real images are unlikely, but not impossible. For example, if one element happens to occlude another in a particular view, then a single element might split and become two elements at a later time. This is a rather rare event, and therefore mappings with splits and fusions should be avoided, but not at all cost. Let δ denote the probability of an occlusion, or any other source of splits and fusions in images. Consequently, the probability of a simple split (an input element in the image splitting to create two output elements) or a simple fusion (two input elements converging onto the same output element) is δ. The probability of an element having three links ("double occlusion") is δ^2. In general, the probability of a split with $s + 1$ links is δ^s, and the probability of a fusion with $f + 1$ links is δ^f. The probability of a match containing k splits with $s_1+1,...,s_k+1$ links, and n fusions with $f_1+1,...,f_n+1$ links, is given by:

$$\Pi\, p(v_i)\, \delta^{s_1}...\delta^{f_n} \tag{12}$$

By taking the -log of the above expression we find that the "cost" of the match (where $\sigma = -\log \delta$) is:

$$\Sigma q(v_i) + \sigma(\Sigma s_i + \Sigma f_j) \quad i = 1,...,k, \quad j = 1,...,n. \tag{13}$$

The optimal match is found by minimizing (13) rather than (3). The larger the σ in this last expression (that is, the smaller the probability of splits and fusions), the higher will be the preference for one-to-one mappings.

There are empirical grounds as well for associating additional penalty with splits and fusions. Figure 3.3 provides an example. The match in Figure 3.3a ($A1{\to}B1{\leftarrow}A2$, $B2{\leftarrow}A3{\to}B3$) minimizes Σq_i (this statement holds for long ISI, see Section 3.6), but the one-to-one match in Figure 3.3b ($A1{\to}B1$, $A2{\to}B2$, $A3{\to}B3$) is perceptually preferred.

This section establishes the perhaps unexpected result that the minimal mapping method can be "tuned" in a very simple way to avoid splits and fusions by any desired amount. The only

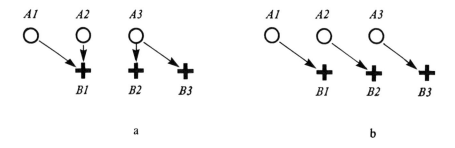

Figure 3.3 Preference for one-to-one mappings. The match in 3.3b is preferred although the total cost in 3.3a is lower.

modification required is the addition of a single constant to the cost function q. The value of this constant is shown to be 2σ (where $\sigma = -\log \delta$, as above).

The modified minimal mapping method

Suppose that rather than minimizing $\Sigma\, q_{ij}x_{ij}$, we now minimize the sum:

$$\Sigma\, q_{ij}x_{ij} + k\Sigma x_{ij} \quad (\text{or, equivalently, } \Sigma\, [k + q_{ij}]x_{ij}\,)$$

As before, in the optimal solution the x_{ij} will be binary, hence the "penalty function" $k\Sigma x_{ij}$ is simply k times the total number of links in the match. By making k larger, mappings with a smaller number of links will be preferred. Furthermore, the next proposition shows that for the appropriate choice of k we can minimize the required sum in (13).

<u>Proposition</u>: Minimizing $\Sigma q_{ij}x_{ij} + 2\sigma\Sigma x_{ij}$ (subject to the usual constraints $\Sigma x_{ij} \geq 1$) is equivalent to minimizing the penalized sum in (13) over all covers.

<u>Proof</u>: First note that chains of corresponding elements are precluded. Examine the chain: $A1 \rightarrow B1 \leftarrow A2 \rightarrow B2$. The link $B1 \leftarrow A2$ can be removed without violating the constraints, hence this chain cannot be part of the optimal solution. Let m be the

number of one-to-one links in a given match. The total number of links in this match is:

$$\Sigma x_{ij} = m + \Sigma(s_i + 1) + \Sigma(f_j + 1) \qquad (14)$$

where i ranges over the splits and j over the fusions. The number of input elements I is given by:

$$I = m + \Sigma|s| + \Sigma(f_j + 1) \qquad (15)$$

where |s| is the total number of splits. The number of output elements O is given by:

$$O = m + \Sigma(s_i + 1) + |f| \qquad (16)$$

where |f| is the total number of fusions. We now subtract $\sigma(I + O)$ from our objective function. This quantity does not depend on the match, therefore it does not alter the minimization problem (i.e. a match minimizes the sum $\Sigma q_{ij}x_{ij} + 2\sigma\Sigma x_{ij}$ if and only if it also minimizes $\Sigma q_{ij}x_{ij} + 2\sigma\Sigma x_{ij} - \sigma(I + O)$). By substituting for Σx_{ij}, I, and O, the penalty $2\sigma\Sigma x_{ij} - \sigma(I + O)$ becomes:

$$\sigma(\Sigma s_i + \Sigma f_j) \qquad (17)$$

Minimizing $\Sigma q_{ij}x_{ij} + 2\sigma\Sigma x_{ij}$ is therefore equivalent to minimizing $\Sigma q_{ij}x_{ij} + \sigma(\Sigma s_i + \Sigma f_j)$. Since the x_{ij} are binary, (and constrained by $\Sigma x_{ij} \geq 1$) this is equivalent to minimizing $\Sigma q_{ij} + \sigma(\Sigma s_i + \Sigma f_j)$ over all covers. ∎

In summary, the penalized sum in (13) can be optimized without affecting the computation described in Section 3.4. The cost q_{ij} can simply subsume the constant k, so that the optimal solution is still found by minimizing $\Sigma q_{ij}x_{ij}$. The responsibility for preferring one-to-one mappings can be distributed throughout the network by simply adding 2σ to the cost function q(v). The computation remains simple and local, while exhibiting the required degree of preference for one-to-one mappings.

To appreciate the implication of this section, consider, for instance, the match between *n* input and *n + 1* output elements. Suppose that the penalty is sufficiently large so that the match will be "as one-to-one as possible", i.e. there will be only a single split. The overall match must include a split, the split must be unique, and the resulting match must minimize the total cost. If an element "decides" to split, it must "make sure" that no other element does. Furthermore, the right element must split, since the wrong element splitting will cause the cost function to be non-optimal. It therefore seems that establishing the correct match will require complex interactions, communication among distant elements, or some global control process that coordinates all the pairings. However the implication of the last two sections is that none of the above is necessary. The optimal match, which will contain a single split, is attainable using only simple, local interactions.

We conclude that the minimal mapping, including the appropriate bias for one-to-one matchings, is computable from the underlying affinities via local interactions. The minimal mapping is thus a workable scheme, which is suggestive as an explanation for the correspondence process employed by the human visual system. It should be noted, however, that the network described above is not advanced as an explicit model. A distinction should be drawn between a model and a computational study of the underlying principles. In an explicit model, a formal description is given, and a claim is made for a direct isomorphism between elements of the model and elements of the system being modeled. The principle objective here was not to model the correspondence process, but to investigate some computational aspects of the problem. The main conclusions of this investigation are that the minimal mapping is, under certain conditions, optimal, and that it is computable from the underlying affinities via the local process in accordance with the scheme described in Chapter 2. According to this view, the role of the interactions examined in Chapter 2 is to increase the total affinity, thus leading to, or at least approximating, the minimal mapping, and thereby establishing the most probable match between the participating tokens. We shall further explore the similarities between the minimal mapping and the human correspondence process in the next section.

3.6 Properties of the Minimal Mapping

Until now we have characterized the optimal correspondence strategy by a certain mathematical condition, namely minimizing a cost function over all the local covers. In this section we turn to the examination of some of the properties of the minimal mapping and compare them, when possible, to properties of the correspondence established by the human visual system.

Minimizing the total distance

As the inter-stimulus interval (ISI) between successive frames increases, the minimal mapping is expected to minimize the total distance covered by all the elements in the image. That is, if d_i is the distance traveled by the ith input element, then the minimal mapping will minimize the quantity Σd_i over the legal matches.

For low velocities, $p(v)$ can be expressed as $p_0 + kv$, where $p_0 = p(0)$, and k is the derivative of $p(v)$ at 0 (we shall see later that $k < 0$). For small v, the following approximation holds:

$$q(v) = -\log p(v) = -\log (p_0 + kv) = \alpha + \beta v \qquad (18)$$

where $\alpha = -\log p_0$, $\beta = -k/p_0$.

If, for example, one-to-one mappings are considered (as will usually be the case), the contribution of α is constant, and the preferred match minimizes the sum of velocities Σv_i. In the case of two frames with high ISI between them, this is also equivalent (since $v_i = d_i * $ ISI) to minimizing the total distance Σd_i [3.8].

The rule of non-crossing trajectories

It has been noticed that the paths of elements in apparent motion seldom cross [Kolers, 1972; Attneave, 1974; Navon, 1976]. If *Al, A2* are shown in apparent motion with *Bl, B2* in a configuration where the paths *Al → B2, A2 → Bl* cross, but *Al → Bl, A2 → B2* do not (Figure 3.4), then the latter match is preferred (provided that the ISI is not too short).

The rule of non-crossing trajectories is implied, at least

in part, by the minimum distance principle. The triangle inequality implies that $(d_1 + d_2) < (c_1 + c_2)$ in Figure 3.4. That is, the non-crossing trajectories always minimize the total distance and therefore, for long ISI, also minimize Σq_i.

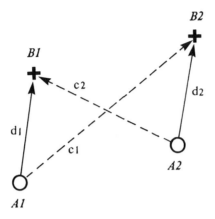

Figure 3.4 Non crossing trajectories. The total distance of the non crossing paths is always smaller that that of the crossing paths.

Kolers [1972, p. 77] provided interesting examples showing that some cases of non-crossing trajectories cannot be accounted for merely on the basis of total distance. He concluded that the visual system "cannot tolerate" crossing trajectories (outside special cases of motion in depth). It does not seem necessary, however, to assume that the visual system explicitly prohibits crossing paths. It should first be noted that, as expected from the minimal mapping, crossing trajectories can be obtained by manipulating the affinities between the participating elements (i.e., if the affinity between $A2$ and $B1$ in Figure 3.4 is sufficiently high). Secondly, grouping effects should sometimes be taken into account as well. I have mentioned in Section 2.4.2 the possibility of grouping elementary tokens into higher order tokens. For example, the dots in Figure 3.5 can be grouped into line segments with associated lengths and orientations. The correspondence in this case can be established either between the individual dots, or between the two group tokens. The different alternatives compete with each other, and the question of which one will prevail depends on various affinity and temporal parameters. This additional competition can be incorporated into the minimal mapping scheme of Sections 3.4 and 3.5. This is a highly important extension. However, since not enough is known about grouping, this extension will not be further discussed. For the present, it will suffice to note that on the basis of various examples I have considered (e.g. examples 22 and 23 in [Kolers 1972]), path-length and grouping are probably sufficient to account for the non-crossing trajectories [3.9].

Figure 3.5   Group tokens. The dots may be grouped into line segments prior to the establishment of a correspondence.

Flow detection

Suppose that two snapshots (S1 and S2) are taken of a collection of elements moving parallel to each other. We shall refer to such a parallel motion as a *flow* of the elements. The visual system seems capable of detecting flows: when the two snapshots S1 and S2 are presented in succession, the flow motion will usually be perceived (provided that the ISI is not too short). This holds true even when the average distance traveled by the elements between the two snapshots is considerably larger than the mean inter-element distance, in which case virtually none of the elements are paired with their nearest neighbors [3.10].

This flow detection capacity deserves a closer examination since it does not appear to be consistent with the independence hypothesis made in Section 3.2. It seems to indicate that each element "prefers" a match whose direction is consistent with the direction of neighboring elements. The independence hypothesis, on the other hand, excluded interactions based on directional similarity. The flow detection phenomenon might also suggest the existence of some global measurements, which do not belong to any single processor in the simple network discussed in Section 3.4. The prevailing orientation could be discovered by a global measurement and could then affect the match assigned to the individual elements. However, such a suggestion concerning interactions between local and global processes runs contrary to the simple network model. The flow detection phenomenon therefore raises the following problem. In a simple network model, the correspondence between collections of elements is governed completely by the local interactions. According to the independence hypothesis, these local interactions do not include positive interactions between matches of similar directions. Yet, when a common direction does exist it seems to affect the correspondence process, as indicated by the flow detection phenomenon.

To resolve this difficulty, we shall turn to an examination of the flow detection in light of the minimal mapping. The conclusion we shall reach is that flow detection is not at odds with either the independence assumption or the simple network model. In fact, it supports them since, as we shall see, the minimal mapping actually implies flow detection.

Recall that S2 is obtained from S1 by translating all the elements along a common direction. The correct match between S1 and S2 is the one in which each element in S1 is paired with its translated image in S2. We now wish to establish:

Claim (the flow-detection lemma):

The correct match minimizes the total distance Σd_i (over all the one-to-one mappings).

Proof:

Let (x_i, y_i) denote the position (in the image plane) of the ith input element, and (x'_i, y'_i) its position in the second snapshot. If the X-axis is chosen to coincide with the direction of the flow, then $y'_i = y_i$, and $x'_i \geq x_i$. A match between the snapshots is a function m which assigns an output element to every input element. Thus $j = m(i)$ means that the jth output element is paired with the ith input element.

The total distance Dc of the correct match is given by:

$$Dc = \Sigma \; (x'_i - x_i), \; = \; \Sigma x'_i - \Sigma x_i \tag{19}$$

For another match m, the total distance Dm is given by:

$$Dm = \Sigma \; [\; (x'_j - x_i)^2 + (y'_j - y_i)^2 \;]^{1/2} \tag{20}$$
$$i = 1,..,n \quad j = m(i).$$

We can now compare the total distance of matches m and c:

$$Dm \geq \Sigma \; |x'_j - x_i| \geq \Sigma \; (x'_j - x_i) = \Sigma \; x'_j - \Sigma x_i = Dc \tag{21}$$
$$i = 1,...,n \quad j = m(i).$$

Since $Dm \geq Dc$, Dc is minimal, and the correct match is optimal.

∎

It can also be seen that Dm will be strictly greater than Dc unless m is also a flow, namely $y'_j = y_i$, $x'_j \geq x_i$. Aside from some special situations the optimal match will therefore be unique.

The flow-detection lemma can also be proven for the case of radial motion. Suppose that each element moves (in the image plane) along the line which connects it to a certain fixed point o. (Such radial flow can arise from an approaching object, as well as from the perspective projection of pure translation in space.) Then, the correct radial correspondence minimizes the total distance.

Proof: Let o be the origin, and describe the position of each element by its polar coordinates (r, θ). If d_{ij} is the distance between input element i and output element j, then $d_{ij} \geq |r_i - r_j|$.

For a given match m,

$$Dm = \Sigma\; d_{ij} \geq \Sigma\; |r_i - r_j| \geq \Sigma\; (r_i - r_j) = Dr \qquad (22)$$
$$i = 1,...,n \quad j = m(i)$$

where Dr is the total distance of the correct (radial) correspondence. ∎

Comments: rotary motion is different, with respect to flow detection, from translatory and radial flow. If S2 is obtained from S1 via a rotation by a sufficient amount, the minimal mapping will not always coincide with the rotation. We can therefore expect that under the appropriate conditions rotary flow (in discrete presentation) will break down at smaller average displacements than translatory and radial flows [3.11]. It should also be mentioned that additional sources might contribute to the perception of coherent motion. If the displacement is small, it might be detected by the short-range process mentioned in Section 1.2. This process would be applicable even when the number of tokens becomes so large as to preclude the establishment of correspondence between all the individual tokens.

The independence hypothesis revisited

The optimal correspondence strategy was developed for independently moving elements. The independence assumption might be questioned on the grounds that proximate elements in the image are likely to move in similar directions. It can be argued, therefore, that if a "locally parallel" match (i.e., a match in which the motion of proximate elements is nearly parallel) exists, it should be preferred. While there is probably some truth to this argument, the flow detection analysis suggests that the explicit incorporation of such a preference would be redundant, since parallel motions also minimize Σd_i. The minimal mapping is thus a plausible method whether or not the motion of the elements is in fact independent. It should also be noted that the minimal mapping method requires only the measurement of distances between elements and not of directions, a property that might have an advantage in terms of economical implementation. Since the number of elements in a scene can be large, a computation of the optimal correspondence based on a minimal number of parameters, and with a minimal number of interactions, might offer an important advantage.

Symmetry

One property of the human correspondence process is "a preference for symmetrical movement, more important things being equal" [Attneave, 1974, p. 118]. Such a symmetry property is to be expected in any simple local network as defined in Section 3.4. Furthermore, if there is a symmetry in the input, then there must be a symmetric optimal match. Symmetry can be defined as a permutation π that "does not alter the problem". That is to say, if q_{ij} is the cost of the link between input element i and output element j, and q'_{ij} is the cost of the link between $\pi(i)$ and $\pi(j)$, then for all i and j, $q_{ij} = q'_{ij}$. If such a symmetry exists, then:

1) There exists a symmetric optimal match, i.e., a match in which $x_{ij} = x'_{ij}$. This holds because if $[x_{ij}]$ (a sequence of 1's and 0's) is an optimal solution, then so is $[x'_{ij}]$. The solution $[y_{ij}]$ defined by $y_{ij} = (x_{ij} + x'_{ij})/2$ is also optimal, and symmetric.
2) The iterative procedure (9) will converge to a symmetric optimal solution (provided that it is a legal match). Since the input is symmetric, the first stage in the iteration is symmetric. Since all the processors are identical, the next stage, and by induction all stages, will be symmetric as well.

The symmetric configurations can be divided into two categories: integer and non-integer. Figure 3.6 exemplifies a non-integer symmetric configuration. Figure 3.6a shows one optimal mapping and Figure 3.6b another. The mapping in Figure 3.6c is a combination of the two, and is both optimal and symmetric. As has been noted in Section 3.4, when (and only when) the optimal solution is not unique, there also exist non-integer optimal solutions, of which Figure 3.6c is an example. The mapping in Figure 3.6c is expected to be unstable, since it relies on the exact equality of the distances *A1-B2*, and *A2-B2*. Any devialotion

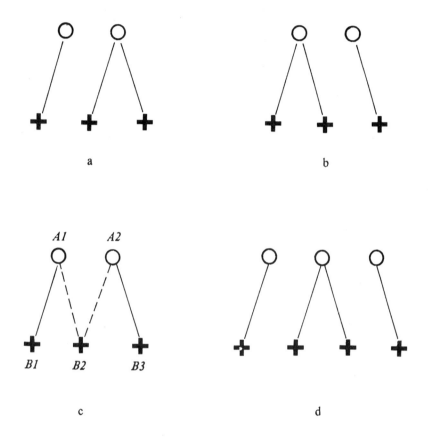

Figure 3.6 Symmetric matches. The match in 3.6c is symmetric, but non-integral and unstable. The match in 3.6d is symmetric, integral, and stable.

from the strict equality between these distances will cause either Figure 3.5a or Figure 3.6b to be optimal. It is not surprising, therefore, that the perception associated with this configuration is unstable and alternates between the two [Kolers, 1972; Attneave, 1974; Section 2.4 of this work].

Figure 3.6d shows an optimal, symmetric, integer mapping. Unlike the non-integer mappings, these are perceptually stable. This stability is not completely predictable from the minimal mapping since it depends on properties of the algorithm by which the method is carried out. It can be verified that if a row of n elements is shown in alternation with a row comprising $n+1$ elements, then whenever n is even the symmetric solution is non-integer, and whenever n is odd there exists a symmetric, optimal, integer solution. It is therefore reasonable to expect that in the first case the perceived match will be unstable and asymmetric, and in the second stable and symmetric. This prediction is consistent with the observations of Kolers [1972] and of Attneave [1974].

Symmetry in the order of presentation

When two frames f1 and f2 are shown in apparent motion, the perceived correspondence does not depend on the order of presentation. That is, the pairing of elements remains the same regardless of whether f1 precedes or follows f2. This symmetry is shared by the minimal mapping correspondence process. The optimal solution to the matching problem remains invariant when the input and output elements switch roles.

The minimal cover property

The minimal mapping is a minimal cover in the sense that it does not contain superfluous links. The removal of any link from the match will result in one input or output element being "uncovered" (i.e., without a counterpart). This property implies the phenomena of split and fusion competition discussed in Section 2.4]. Figure 3.7 illustrates the split competition. In Figure 3.7a, element Al is presented followed by a pair of flanking elements *B1* and *B2*. *A1* is perceived as splitting and matching both *B1* and *B2*. In Figure 3.7b, a second element, *A2*, is added to the first frame. The resulting correspondence is *A1* → *B1*, *A2* → *B2*, while the link *A1* → *B2* disappears. It is as if *A2*, by taking over *B2*, competes with *A1* and prevents it from matching *B2*. In the minimal mapping the three links *A1* → *B1*, *A1* → *B2*, *A2* → *B2*, cannot coexist since this mapping will not be a minimal cover (*A1* → *B2* is removable). Similarly, Attneave

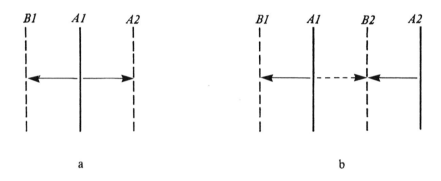

a   b

Figure 3.7 The minimal cover property. In 3.7b A1 will not split since the link A1 → B1 would be superfluous.

[1974] described configurations in apparent motion where the number of links is kept to the minimum required to supply each element with a partner. Observing this minimal cover property as well as such properties as symmetry and non-crossing paths, Attneave [1974] commented:

> "*It would appear that the system is exhibiting foresight, and one is strongly tempted to invoke some "deus ex machina", some superordinate, ratiomorphic control system that makes everything come out neatly*" [Attneave, 1974, p. 116].

The discussion in the preceeding sections establishes that no such global planning is required. A simple, local process can possess all the discussed properties, and is in fact expected to exhibit them if it computes the minimal mapping.

Monotonicity in the rate of sampling

Roughly speaking, if the min Σd_i mapping yields the correct correspondence when the second view is separated by a time interval t from the first, then for every $t' < t$ the match will also be correct.

To prove the above claim, we shall assume that the elements are moving along straight lines (an assumption which will hold for short time intervals). Two snapshots of the moving elements separated by a time interval t are given. Suppose that the correct match (i.e., the match in which each input element is paired with the same element after the time interval t) minimizes Σd_i. Then, for every $t' < t$, the correct correspondence will also minimize Σd_i.

Proof:

Let v_i be the velocity of the ith element, σ will denote the total distance Σd_i of the correct match at time t, and σ' the total distance at time t'. Let μ' be the total distance Σd_i of some one-to-one match m' at time interval t'. We wish to establish that $\sigma' \leq \mu'$. From the match m' at time t' one can obtain a match m at time t: if a point x is paired by m with some point y(t') (i.e., point y at time t'), then m is obtained by pairing x with y(t). Figure 3.8 represents the different matches. The correct match is $y(0) \rightarrow y(t') \rightarrow y(t)$. In m' x(0) $\rightarrow$ y(t'), and in m x(0) $\rightarrow$ y(t). We shall denote by μ the total distance of the new match m. From the assumption that the correct match minimizes Σd_i at time t, $\sigma \leq \mu$. To prove our claim, it is therefore sufficient to show that $\sigma - \sigma' \geq \mu - \mu'$. To do so, return to Figure 3.8. The contribution of element y to σ is $v_y t$ and its contribution to σ' is $v_y t'$. The difference between the two contributions is $v_y*(t - t')$, which is the segment r in Figure 3.8. In match m, x $\rightarrow$ y(t) and in m', x $\rightarrow$ y(t'). The difference between the two contributions

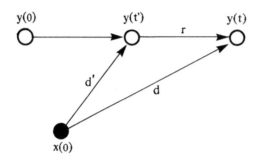

Figure 3.8 Monotonicity in the rate of sampling. The correct match is
y(0) → y(t') → y(t). In match *m'*, x(0) → y(t'). In match *m*, x(0) → y(t).

of y is (d - d') in Figure 3.8, and (d - d') ≤ r (the triangle
inequality). Similar inequalities hold for all the elements, hence
$\mu - \mu' \leq \sigma - \sigma'$. Combined with the known inequality $\sigma \leq \mu$, the
implication is that $\sigma' \leq \mu'$, that is, σ' is minimal. ∎

The monotonicity property has possible application for
the correspondence computation; for example, in eliminating
wrong matches by checking for consistency with intermediate
matches. Suppose that an element x in S1 is matched with y in
a subsequent frame S2, and z in a third frame S3. If the correspondence is correct, the matches must be consistent, i.e., y → z.
Figure 3.9 shows an inconsistent match: the correspondence
process paired x → y, x → z, but y → w. By accepting only consistent matches, the correspondence process can reduce the
number of wrong matches. Such a consistency check can be
performed for any correspondence scheme, regardless of monotonicity. However the monotonicity implies that "false alarms",

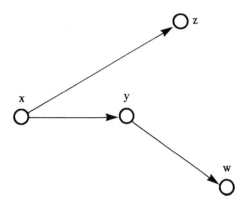

Figure 3.9 An inconsistent match. x → y, x → z, but y → w.

in which x → z is correct but the match is rejected, are highly
unlikely.   Observations of the human correspondence process
suggest that the human visual system does not use such consistency verifications. However, it seems that, in accordance with
the monotonicity property, the performance of the human correspondence apparatus improves monotonically with the rate of
sampling.

The shape of q(v) and some of its implications

The preference for nearest neighbors
         It has been frequently noted that the human correspond-
ence process tends to match each element with its nearest
neighbor, whenever such a choice is possible without violating
other conditions. For example, in Figure 3.10a, element Z can
be paired with either $Y1$ or $Y2$. Both matches will be legal, since
each of the input elements (X, V, Z) is paired with at least one
output element, and each of the output elements $(Y1, Y2)$ is
paired with at least one input elements in both matches. In such
a situation the matching of Z with its nearest neighbor will
always be preferred. That is, if $d_1 < d_2$ in Figure 3.10a, the

match $Z \to Y1$ will be preferred over $Z \to Y2$. In Figure 3.10b, on the other hand, Z will match $Y2$, since a match with its nearest neighbor $Y1$ will produce an illegal match.

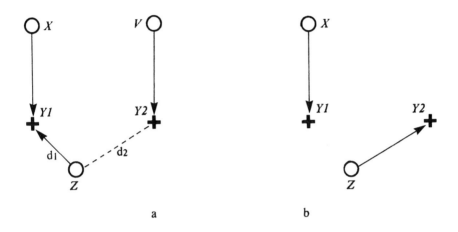

Figure 3.10 Preference for the nearest neighbor. Unlike 3.10a, in 3.10b Z is not paired with its nearest neighbor, since the resulting match will not be a minimal cover.

The preference for the nearest neighbor might seem to suggest that the correspondence process incorporates the assumption that lower velocities are more probable than higher ones. At the low velocity end this assumption seems dubious: while very high velocities are unlikely, there is no reason to assume that a velocity of, say 1.0 degree/second is significantly more (or less) frequent than a velocity of, say, 0.5 degree/second. What might, then, account for the strong preference for nearest neighbors at all velocities?

The answer is that, in the framework of the minimal mapping, the nearest neighbor should be strongly preferred almost independent of the probability distribution of velocities in the environment. Recall that q(v), the function to be minimized by the correspondence process, was defined as -log p(v), where p(v) is the probability distribution of velocities in the image plane. Let $\rho(v)$ denote the probability distribution of the velocity of the elements in space. That is to say, if a moving element is selected at random, the probability that its velocity (in space) v lies between values a and b is $\int_a^b \rho(u)du$. Assuming spatial isotropy (i.e., that the elements have equal probabilities of moving in any direction in space), the probability distribution of the velocity in the image plane is proportional to:

$$\int_v^\infty \rho(u) \, (u^2 - v^2)^{-1/2} \, du \qquad (23)$$

(This expression holds for orthographic projection. The change required for perspective projection is insignificant [3.12].) The preference of p(v) for nearest neighbors is considerably stronger than that of $\rho(v)$. If the function $\rho(v)$ is monotonically decreasing, so is p(v). However, p(v) can prefer nearest neighbors even if, for example, at the low velocity range higher velocities are more probable (in 3-D space) than lower ones. The underlying reason lies in the relation between velocities in space and projected velocities. If the projected velocity is v, the actual velocity u in space must have been at least equal to v, but could have been any higher velocity. Consequently, the smaller the projected velocity, the larger is the set of spatial velocities that can produce it. Figure 3.11 shows an example where $\rho(v)$ is taken to be first increasing, then decreasing. The function p(v), on the other hand, computed via (23), induces a marked preference for nearest neighbors at all velocities.

If p(v) is monotonically decreasing, then an obvious simple correspondence strategy that suggests itself is the nearest-neighbor match in which, given two frames, each element in one frame is paired with its nearest neighbor in the other. Indeed, for sufficiently low velocities, where the nearest-neighbor match induces one-to-one mappings, the minimal mapping coincides with the nearest-neighbor match. At higher velocities, the nearest-neighbor match ceases to be optimal, since it often deviates from one-to-one mappings, leading instead to a profusion of splits and fusions. The minimal mapping improves

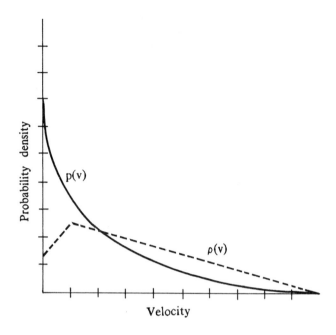

Figure 3.11 Probability distributions of velocity in space (dashed line) and projected velocity (solid line). The projected velocity induces a marked preference for nearest neighbors.

upon the nearest-neighbor match in two ways. First, rather than minimizing the distances themselves, it minimizes a cost function of the distances. As we have seen, the two coincide only at the low velocity end, while at higher velocities the distances are no longer a faithful measure of the match likelihood. Second, it combines the minimization with the required degree of preference for one-to-one mappings. The minimal mapping can thus be viewed as an improvement on the nearest-neighbor match, that extends the range of velocities over which the mapping is applicable. We have mentioned that the convergence of the minimal mapping is global, but the speed of convergence depends on the starting point. To accelerate the convergence, the nearest neighbor match can serve as a plausible starting point; subsequent iterations will then improve the match, driving it towards the minimal mapping.

Ternus' configuration and the sigmoid shape of q(v)

Ternus' configuration in apparent motion has been introduced in Section 2.4. It is composed of two dots (*A* and *B)* presented in brief succession with a second pair (*B, C)*. Dots *A, B*, and *C* lie in the same horizontal row. Depending on various conditions, the perceived correspondence can be in one of two modes. In the "coherent" mode the pair (*A, B)* moves as a unit to the right (i.e., the perceived correspondence is $A \to B, B \to C)$. In the "neighbor" mode $B \to B$, while *A* often "jumps over" to match *C.*

If the function $q(v)$ is convex for low velocities, the minimal mapping would imply the coherent mode of correspondence in the low velocity region. In the coherent mode the distances of the match are both equal to d. In the neighbor mode, one of the distances is 0, the other is 2d. The convexity of $q(v)$ would imply that:

$$q(0) + q(2d) > 2q(d) \qquad (24)$$

Hence, the coherent mode minimizes $\Sigma \, q_i$.

As we shall see, there is reason to believe that in the high velocity region $q(v)$ is concave. The function $q(v)$ thus assumes a sigmoid shape, as diagrammed in Figure 3.12. The sigmoid shape of $q(v)$ implies that when v is sufficiently large, the minimal method will prefer the neighbor mode over the coherent mode. Figure 3.12 (thin line) depicts the transition point between the two modes, where $q(0) + q(2d) = 2q(d)$. Similarly, the sigmoid shape correctly predicts that crossing trajectories in which one path is longer than the other will be easier to obtain as the velocity increases. Additional aspects of bistable displays support the foregoing account of the Ternus configuration. Consider for instance the configuration in Figure 3.13, where $d_1 + d_2$ equals twice the distance d_3. This display is bistable and

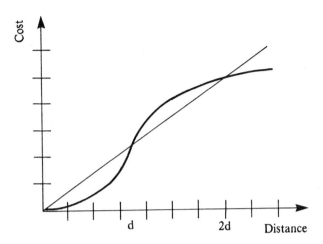

Figure 3.12 The sigmoid shape of $q(v)$ may give rise to the mode transition in Ternus' configuration.

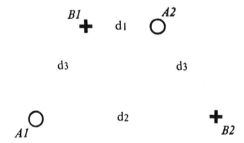

Figure 3.13 A bi-stable configuration. The total distance in the two modes is the same: $d_1 + d_2 = 2d_3$.

exhibits two modes of correspondence. At short ISI the prevailing mode is *A1* → *B2, A2* → *B1*, while at long ISI the match *A1* → *B1, A2* → *B2*, predominates. Unlike the Ternus configuration, the modes in this case cannot be categorized as "element" vs. "group" motions [Pantle and Picciano, 1976]. However, from the standpoint of the minimal mapping, this new configuration is similar to the Ternus configuration. If the total distance of the two modes is the same, the sigmoid shape of q(v) implies a preference for the equal distances mode in the convex region, but for dissimilar distances in the concave region. Note also that if the element *B* in Ternus' configuration is displaced by a distance *h* to the left between presentations, the total distance of the coherent mode decreases (by 2*h*) while the total distance of the neighbor mode remains unchanged. As predicted by the minimal mapping, in this version of the Ternus configuration the preference for the coherent mode increases with *h*.

3.7 The Experimental Determination of q(v)

The optimal match between two collections of points is determined by the function q(v). (q(v) can include the constant k of the modified minimal mapping.) If the visual system incorporates a correspondence method similar to the minimal mapping, is it possible to recover the function q(v) used by the visual system? In other words: Can q(v) be determined *uniquely* by examining the matches established by the visual system? Suppose for instance that a function q'(v) exists, which always predicts the same matches as q(v) (i.e., $\Sigma q'_i$ is minimal whenever Σq_i is). Such a function q'(v) would be indistinguishable from q(v). However, it is possible to show that q(v) can in principle be determined up to a single scaling factor, and that if only one-to-one mappings are examined, q'(v) is indistinguishable from q(v) if and only if q'(v) = aq(v) + b for some constants a and b. That is, by examining one-to-one matches, q(v) can be determined up to a linear function. The following procedure exemplifies how q(v) can be so determined.

We shall make use of bistable displays, similar to the Ternus configuration. If a bistable configuration has two equally probable matches m and m', then $\Sigma q_i = \Sigma q'_i$, where Σq_i is the total cost of m and $\Sigma q'_i$ of m'. In the Ternus configuration, when the transition between the modes occurs, then:

$$\hat{q}(0) + \hat{q}(2v_1) = \hat{q}(v_1) + \hat{q}(v_1) \qquad (25)$$

Let us arbitrarily set $\hat{q}(0)$ to 0, and $\hat{q}(v_1)$ to 1. Consequently, $\hat{q}(2v_1) = 2$. The notation $\hat{q}(v)$ rather than $q(v)$ has been used to draw a distinction between the function $\hat{q}(v)$ (which is determined by the bistable configurations with $\hat{q}(0) = 0$ and $\hat{q}(v_1) = 1$) and the true function $q(v)$ that we are seeking. We can now use v_1 and $v_2 = 2v_1$ to determine new values of $\hat{q}(v)$. For example, in Figure 3.13 we can change d_3 selectively while maintaining d_1 and d_2 fixed, until a bistable configuration is reached (i.e., until $A1 \rightarrow B1$, $A2 \rightarrow B2$, and $A1 \rightarrow B2$, $A2 \rightarrow B1$, are equally probable. To counteract grouping effects, the introduction of background elements might be required.) When this condition is reached, then $\hat{q}(v_1) + \hat{q}(v_2) = \hat{q}(v_3) + \hat{q}(v_3)$. Hence, $\hat{q}(v_3)$ is also determined [3.13]. Theoretically, this method can be extended to determine $q(v)$ on a dense set of values (i.e. between any two known values it is possible to get another value). The function $\hat{q}(v)$ can therefore be measured. We now return to our original function $q(v)$, which must be a linear function of $\hat{q}(v)$, that is $q = a\hat{q} + b$. To determine the additive constant we can use bistable configurations in which the total number of paired elements is different in the two possible matches. Figure 3.14 is an example of such a configuration. By gradually increasing the horizontal distance (h in Figure 3.14) while keeping the other distances constant, the dominant correspondence pattern will shift from 3.14a through 3.14b to 3.14c. Note that when $h = 2v$ patterns 3.14b and 3.14c have the same total length. If the cost function did not include a penalty factor, then, for low velocities (long ISI and presentation time) the total cost would also be the same (Section 3.6). This would result in a multi-stable configuration, in which configurations b1, b2 and c would be of equal likelihood. In fact, under the above conditions the patterns in 3.14b predominate, and *h* has to be greater than 2*v* to obtain multistability. The implication is that a penalty factor is probably incorporated in the cost function, thereby biasing the correspondence towards the match with the least number of links.

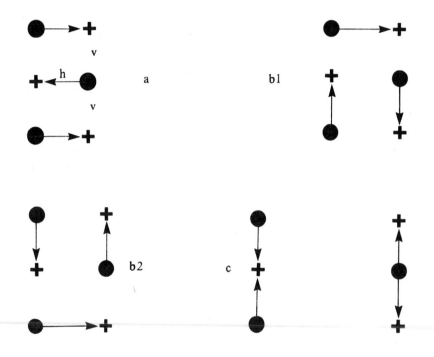

Figure 3.14 As the horizontal distance *h* increases, the dominant correspondence pattern shift from a to b and finally to c. The total number of links is different in patterns b and c.

When the patterns in 3.14b and 3.14c are equally likely, then:

$$q(v) + q(v) + q(v) + q(v) = q(v) + q(v) + q(h)$$
(26)

Substituting $q = a\hat{q} + b$, we get:

$$2\hat{q}(v_2) + b/a + = \hat{q}(h)$$

$\hat{q}(v)$ and $\hat{q}(h)$ are already known, so b/a is determined as well. Since q can be determined only up to a scaling factor, we conclude that $q = c(\hat{q} + b/a,)$ where c is an arbitrary constant.

Other experimental procedures might also serve for the determination of q(v). The relevant point is, however, that q(v) can in principle be determined (up to a scaling factor) on the basis of the matches established by the visual system. Some preliminary exploration of the q(v) function I have conducted fits within the framework outlined so far. However, more elaborate experimentation will be required to determine more precisely the shape of the cost as a function of the velocity, and to determine its dependency on other parameters, as discussed in the next section.

3.8 Extensions

The discussion thus far has concentrated on the correspondence between two frames, each containing dots of equal intensity. In this section the notion of seeking the most likely match between elements via a simple, local process will be extended to include various types of elements and continuous motion.

3.8.1 Extending the Set of Elements

As described in Chapters 1 and 2, the set of basic elements matched by the correspondence process includes such units as edge fragments, line segments, and blobs. The main novelty introduced by extending the set of basic elements is that the optimal mapping is no longer determined by time intervals and distances alone. The likelihood of a match between two elements is influenced in the general case by other parameters, such as orientation, length, and contrast. These parameters influence the likelihood of the match between two given elements, and therefore enter the correspondence process via the "cost" function q. In the human visual system, q might also be affected by the position in the visual field, as indicated by the peripheral increase and the peripheral equation effects described in Chapter 2. However the optimal mapping still minimizes $\Sigma(q_{ij} + k)x_{ij}$, and can be determined by the local computation discussed in Section 3.4. Equivalently, if the affinity is a measure of the likelihoods of various matches (as explained in Section 3.4), then the optimal mapping is obtained in the general case by maximizing the total affinity.

Some empirical evidence supports the view that (1) the match selected by the human correspondence process can indeed be predicted on the basis of maximizing the total affinity, and (2) the relative effect of the various affinity parameters is consistent with likelihood considerations.

Examples of (1):
The likelihood of crossing trajectories (Section 3.6) increases if the elements across the diagonal, but not along the sides, are identical. Similarly, one can selectively favor the neighbor or the coherent mode in Ternus' configuration by manipulating the similarity (in terms of orientation, length, and intensity) of the participating elements [Fernberger, 1934]. Another interesting property of Ternus' configuration that is in accordance with minimum cost (maximum affinity) considerations, is the effect of similarity between frames: a decrease in the similarity between frames reinforces the coherent mode. If, for instance, the first frame is composed of two vertical bars and the second of two horizontal bars, the coherent mode is stronger than in the standard Ternus configuration where all the elements are identical. Pantle and Picciano [1976] found that a contrast reversal (dark dots in the first frame, light in the second) had a similar effect of reinforcing the coherent mode, and this might also be the result of decreasing similarity (although grouping might also contribute to the effect). Figure 3.15 illustrates schematically the effect of the additional dissimilarity on the cost function q. In the standard Ternus configuration the total cost of the neighbor mode (taking q to be a function of v only) is $q(0) + q(2v)$. The total cost of the coherent mode is $q(v) +$

q(v). In the dissimilar case the elements of the second frame are separated from the elements of the first not only in space, but also along another dimension, e.g. orientation or contrast. In

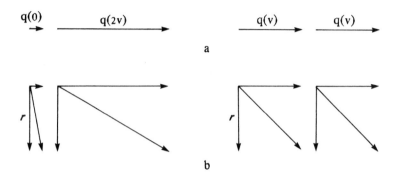

Figure 3.15 Dissimilarity between frames enhances the coherent mode. The vector *r* represents the additional cost due to the dissimilarity.

Figure 3.15b I suggest that the additional separation can be viewed as adding a constant vector *r* along a different dimension to the original distances. (The argument does not depend upon the different dimensions being mutually orthogonal as in the figure.) It is not difficult to verify that as a result of the additional separation $q_1 + q_2 > q_3 + q_4$, hence the coherent mode now minimizes the total cost.

Example of (2):
Table 2.1 suggested that the affinity between short line segments depends on their angular separation in space. Given the isotropy of space, this relation is to be expected if the cost function is

indeed a measure of the relative probability of matches.

3.8.2 Continuous Motion

The goal of this section is to extend the analysis from the discrete presentation of two frames to continuous motion. We shall see that the optimal solution can be established in the continuous case as well by a simple network. The network that carries out this computation is a simple extension of the one described in Section 3.4, and reduces to the previous network in the case of discrete presentation [3.14].

In the continuous case time varies continuously, but we can assume that the location of the elements does not. Namely, that elements can be detected at discrete locations in the image. Unlike the discrete case, the appearance and disappearance of the elements at different locations is no longer synchronized. We shall consider the case of n elements moving about between times $t = t_0$ and $t = T$. As an introduction to the general case we shall make the assumption that at $t = t_0$ and $t = T$ all n elements are detected in the image.

The legal matches in this case are the following. Each of the n elements at $t = t_0$ has one link connecting it to a later element (i.e., an element that appears at a later time). Each of the n elements at $t = T$ has one link connecting it to an earlier element. Each intermediate element has two links, one to an earlier, the other to a later element. By the independence hypothesis, the optimal match is the one that minimizes Σq_i over the legal matches (where i ranges over all the links in the match).

In the two-frame situation the correspondence was equivalent to a cover problem on a bipartite graph, with the bipartite structure playing a pivotal role in determining the local structure of the computation. We shall now formulate the continuous correspondence as a covering of a bipartite graph, and establish the local structure of the continuous correspondence computation. We shall view each element as a pair, composed of a "source" and a "sink". The sources are responsible for establishing connections with later elements, the sinks with earlier elements. Each source has as its initial candidates all the later sinks within a certain spatial neighborhood. The graph of possible pairings now becomes bipartite, the set of all sources being one component, and the set of all sinks the other. As before, the optimal match can be found by:

(27)

Minimize $\Sigma q_{ij} x_{ij}$
Subject to $\Sigma x_{ij} \geq 1$ for every i, where i ranges over all the sources, and
$\Sigma x_{ij} \geq 1$ for every j, where j ranges over all the sinks.

Again, the problem so formulated is equivalent to the optimal correspondence problem provided that $x_{ij} = 1$ if the ith source is matched with the jth sink, and $x_{ij} = 0$ otherwise. Since on a bipartite graph the x_{ij} are guaranteed to be binary, the formulations are equivalent. It is also possible to bias the optimal match towards a minimal number of connections by replacing q_{ij} by $(q_{ij} + k)$ as was done previously. The problem is then formally identical to that of Section 3.4. Hence, the local process (in equations 8 and 9) will converge to the optimal match.

In continuous motion correspondence, the cost function q depends, in addition to the parameters mentioned so far, on their separation *in time*. As might be expected, for the visual system, q_{ij} (the cost of the link between elements i and j) increases with the time interval that separates them. Other parameters (including velocity) being equal, the match that minimizes separation in time will be preferred. For example, the match between two elements separated by a distance *d* and time interval *t*, is stronger than the match between two elements separated by a distance 2*d* and time interval 2*t*. The likelihood of a match between a pair of elements, which is inversely related to the cost q, decreases with the time interval separating the elements. If this time interval exceeds some upper limit τ, the two elements are no longer considered candidates for a match. Rather than having a common time interval within which correspondence is established (the interval to - T in the previous example), each element has as potential matches only the elements within a time interval τ. In such a network there is no "first" or "final" snapshot; the optimal correspondence is computed continuously as the input elements are streaming in.

3.9 On the Relations Between Chapters 2 and 3

Chapters 2 and 3 both examined the correspondence process, but from different approaches. It is of interest to review the relations between the two chapters, with a view towards some general comparisons between the different approaches they represent.

Chapter 2 concentrated on a fairly straightforward examination and interpretation of the observable behavior of the human correspondence process. Such a study eventually faces two difficult problems. The first concerns the unraveling of a process via its overall input-output behavior. For complex processes such a direct investigation might prove impractical, if not impossible. For example, for a process composed of a sequence of operations (e.g. a computer program) the most parsimonious and coherent description might be in terms of these elementary operations. Similarly, for the description of the correspondence process to be manageable, it will probably be necessary to identify its basic components and the interactions among them. But how can one unravel the internal workings of a complex process? (There are methods for investigating "black boxes" if the process is linear, but only some limited methods for classes of non-linear systems.) If the process can be viewed as solving a computational problem, a plausible approach is to seek useful leads by studying the computational problem. This study includes specifying the goal of the computation, and then investigating possible methods for attaining this goal. Suppose, for example, that an investigator is presented with the task of determining the internal mechanisms of an electronic calculator. If the investigator knows that the device is used for performing arithmetic operations, he will have a useful lead to guide his investigation. Without this lead, the investigation might prove intractable.

A second problem with the approach undertaken in Chapter 2 is related to the sort of understanding one seeks. As noted in the introduction, a theory of what is being computed is an integral part of the understanding of information processing systems. With regard to the correspondence process, one might ask, for example, not only what is the form of the competition interactions described in Chapter 2, but also what they accomplish. The computational study is thus aimed at supplementing, as well as directing, the experimental approach. It is also guided, of course, by the experimental data, just as Chapter 3 was motivated and guided by the results of Chapter 2.

In conclusion, let me recapitulate the overall view of the correspondence scheme that arises from Chapters 2 and 3 combined. The input image is processed to form elementary tokens prior to the establishment of correspondence. For the correspondence process, the changing image can then be represented as a stream of incoming tokens. A minimal mapping, which implies the most likely match, is continuously established between the arriving tokens. The basis for the match is the affinity function of Chapter 2 or, in an alternative formulation, the cost function of Chapter 3. The cost function reflects certain "statistics of the universe" [3.15]; it measures the relative probability of different pairings, and is also responsible for biasing the match towards one-to-one mappings by the appropriate amount. The effect of the local interactions is then to minimize the total cost (including a "penalty" for deviations from one-to-one mappings), and thereby optimizing the match.

PART II

THREE-DIMENSIONAL INTERPRETATION

SYNOPSIS

Once the different views representing the same physical object have been matched by the correspondence process, the next step is the interpretation of the 2-D transformations in the object's appearance. The interpretation includes the decomposition of the changing scene into objects, and the recovery of their 3-D structure, motion, and change. Two distinct interpretation processes, the *Structure from Motion* process (abbreviated S.f.M) and the *Motion from Structure* process (M.f.S), are identified and examined in Chapters 4 and 5 respectively.

Chapter 4. The human visual system incorporates a remarkable capacity for correctly interpreting the changing projections of unrecognizable objects in motion. Chapter 4 begins with a computational investigation of the interpretation problem, asking how such a task *can* be accomplished. The results of this investigation then serve to construct a scheme for the interpretation of structure from the changing image of objects in motion.

Section 4.1 defines the structure from motion interpretation problem. It describes the *two cylinders* demonstration, which illustrates the capacity of the human visual system to infer 3-D structure from a changing image, even when each static projection by itself contains no 3-D information.
Section 4.2 examines three explanations that have been offered in the past for the interpretation process. They include the estimation of depth through velocity, the association of kinetic depth with certain "determinants", and Gibson's "immediate perception".
Section 4.3 argues that additional information is required to

constrain the interpretation task, and introduces the notion of *reflective constraints.*

Section 4.4 suggests the *rigidity assumption* as the reflective constraint for the interpretation of structure from motion. The analysis of the rigidity assumption is based primarily on the structure-from-motion theorem, which states that the structure of four non-coplanar points is uniquely recoverable from three orthographic projections. The results are used to develop a scheme that can actually perform the interpretation task. The interpretation is accomplished by the scheme without any need for familiarity with, or recognition of, the objects in the scene.

Section 4.5 extends the analysis from parallel to perspective projections. Two extensions are considered: the direct perspective method, which takes into account the different underlying geometry (Section 4.5.1), and the polar-parallel method, which uses the parallel scheme to obtain local approximations for the perspective case (Section 4.5.2). Theoretical considerations as well as experimental data suggest that the interpretation process incorporated in the human visual system is based on principles similar to those of the polar-parallel scheme.

Section 4.6 reviews relevant experimental findings, in order to examine the applicability of the rigidity based scheme as a psychological theory for the perception of structure from motion.

Chapter 5. In this chapter a second interpretation process, the *motion from structure* (M.f.S) scheme, is discussed. The M.f.S process participates in the interpretation of spatial motion but, unlike the S.f.M scheme, it requires that the 3-D structure of the scene be perceivable from the static projections.

Section 5.1 provides evidence in support of the existence of the M.f.S process and explores some of its properties. Unlike the S.f.M scheme of the previous chapter, the M.f.S process relies on a static 3-D description of the portrayed scene. From the 3-D "labels" assigned to elements in successive views, spatial motion is inferred and "filled-in".

Section 5.2 examines various phenomena related to the "Ames window" illusion. It serves as a conclusion for the second part of the work by bringing together various aspects of the two interpretation schemes.

CHAPTER 4

THE INTERPRETATION OF STRUCTURE FROM MOTION

4.1 Structure from Parallel Projection

Once a correspondence has been established, the next stage concerns the interpretation of the resulting 2-D transformations in terms of the 3-D structure and motion of the viewed objects.

An extreme empiricist approach to the interpretation problem might try to account for the interpretation in terms of past experience with the object in question, or with similar objects. Thus, when one sees, say, a rotating cube, one recognizes its different views on the basis of past experience as representing the same cube from different viewing angles. However, the insufficiency of such an empiricist explanation is demonstrated by the fact that the image of moving objects can be interpreted correctly even when the objects are unfamiliar, and when each static view of the scene contains no information at all about the 3-D structure of the objects. This intriguing capacity of the human visual system to interpret the structure and motion of unrecognizable objects has been the subject of numerous psychological studies [4.1]. Its first systematic examination was carried out by Wallach and O'Connell [1953] in the study of what they have termed the "kinetic depth effect" (KDE). In their experiments, an unfamiliar object was rotated behind a translucent screen, and the shadow of its parallel projection observed from the other side of the screen. (The term "parallel projection" will be used throughout this chapter interchangeably with orthographic projection, to mean a projection by parallel rays that are perpendicular to the image plane.) In most cases the viewers were able to give a correct description of the hidden object's structure and motion, even when each static view of the object was unrecognizable.

The original kinetic depth experiments employed primarily wireframe objects whose projection consisted of a connected set of line segments. Later studies [e.g. Wallach & O'Connell, 1953; White & Mueser, 1960; Green, 1961; Braunstein, 1962; Johansson, 1974, 1975] have established that 3-D structure can be perceived from displays consisting of unconnected elements in motion. (The term "elements" will be used to denote any identifiable feature points, such as isolated points, terminations of line segments, or texture elements.) Such displays have typically employed a small number of elements (one in [von Hofsten, 1974], two in [Borjesson & von Hofsten, 1972], three in [Borjesson & von Hofsten, 1973], up to six in [Braunstein, 1962]); or elements confined to planar surfaces [Gibson & Gibson, 1957; von Fieandt & Gibson, 1959; Gibson *et al* 1959; Gibson, 1965]. In the next section, a demonstration that extends the above demonstrations somewhat by using a large number of points arranged in two non-planar configurations is described. It will exemplify the perception of structure from motion, and will set the stage for formulating the computational problems underlying this perception.

The two cylinders demonstration

The orthographic projection of two coaxial cylinders was presented on a computer-controlled CRT screen. Each cylinder was defined solely by 100 points lying on its surface. The common axis of the two cylinders was vertical, as diagrammed in Figure 4.1. The 3-D coordinates of the points were stored in the computer's memory; their orthographic projection on the frontal plane was computed and presented on the screen. The imaginary cylinders were then rotated (up to about 10 degrees at a time), and their new projection was computed and displayed on the screen (presentation time being 100 msec. with 40 msec. ISI). In the projected image the dots increased in density at the edges of each cylinder, but in the combined image of the two cylinders the variations in density were complex and ineffective in revealing the 3-D structure of the displayed objects. Each single

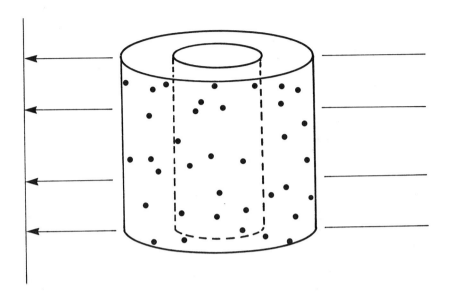

Figure 4.1 The projection of the two cylinders: a side view. The outlines of
the cylinders were not presented in the actual display.

static view thus appeared almost as a random collection of
points. However, when the changing projection was viewed, the
elements in motion across the screen were perceived as two
rotating cylinders whose shapes and angles of rotation were
easily determined. Both the segmentation of the scene into
objects and the 3-D interpretation were based in this case on
motion alone, since each single view contained no information
concerning the segmentation or the structure. Each frame in the
presentation was an unfamiliar, unrecognizable view of the two
cylinders, indicating that familiarity and recognition are not
prerequisites for the interpretation of motion.

Two restrictions of the above demonstration are noteworthy. First, the rotation axis employed in the demonstration
was fixed in space throughout the motion. However, similar
demonstrations, in which the orientation of the rotation axis
changed abruptly (by 30 degrees and more) after each frame,

were examined as well, and the 3-D structure was still perceptible (c.f. the "tumbling motion" in [Green, 1961]). Second, the demonstration employed discrete stimuli in apparent motion. This appears, however, to be immaterial for the interpretation process. Three-dimensional structure can be perceived from both continuous and apparent motion, and the subsequent analysis will be applicable to both.

To summarize, the problem of interpreting structure from motion includes the decomposition of a changing image into the objects in the scene, and the recovery of their 3-D structure and spatial motion, even when no 3-D information is conveyed by a single view.

The term "spatial motion" means here a transformation (rotation followed by translation) which will carry a given object from one known position to another. The term "structure" above is to be distinguished from absolute depth. Only the relative internal depths are to be recovered. Both the actual size and distance might remain undetermined, but all the internal distances within an object are to be determined up to a single scaling factor. (In other words, there is no way of distinguishing between the monocular projections of a small nearby object and a far-away but proportionally larger one; see also Appendix 2.)

The objective of this chapter is to examine the computational problems underlying the interpretation of structure from motion, and to develop a scheme that can actually perform this interpretation. Given the projection of the two cylinders, for example, it will decompose the scene into the two objects and recover their correct 3-D structure as well as their motions in space. Before presenting the solution, three types of explanations that have been offered in the past but seem inadequate will be briefly discussed. This criticism will serve as a vehicle for making several points concerning the study of visual perception in general.

4.2 Criticism of Past Approaches

One approach to the S.f.M interpretation problem has been to estimate the actual depth of individual points on the basis of their velocity: the higher the velocity of an element, the closer it is [Helmholtz, 1910; Braunstein, 1962; Hershberger & Starzec, 1974]. According to this view the recovery of structure from motion is analogous to depth perception through stereopsis. The general idea is to substitute successive frames (motion perception) for concurrent ones (stereopsis), allowing the correspondence process to play the role of binocular fusion, and displacement values the role of disparity. Beyond some special situations (e.g., pure translation of the observer in a stationary environment), this scheme cannot be correct since in the general case displacement values (or, equivalently, velocities) are not indicative of depth. The scene might include objects moving in different directions and at various speeds with no correlation between velocity (or displacement) and depth. Consider also the following "conveyor belt" demonstration which tests the effect of differences in velocity on perceived depth. In this demonstration dots and short line segments move across three regions a, b and c, on a CRT screen, with the boundaries between regions not depicted on the screen (Figure 4.2a). In region b the velocity is v, in a and c it is v', where v' < v. The display simulates the conveyor belt whose top view is illustrated in Figure 4.2b, observed from a frontal view. What perception should arise? The displacement theory predicts that a and c will be seen in one frontal plane, b in another. Another possibility is that the conveyor belt configuration will be seen, in which the real velocity of the elements is constant along their paths [4.2]. Neither expectation is supported by the empirical results. The elements are perceived to move in a frontal plane, accelerating upon their entry to b and decelerating upon leaving it [4.3]. In the two-cylinders example, while velocity cannot serve as an indication of depth, it is true that within each cylinder velocity changes in accordance with depth. It might therefore be

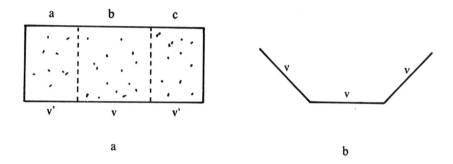

Figure 4.2 The conveyor belt demonstration. The frontal view in 4.2a depicts elements moving at a constatnt velocity along the "conveyor belt" shown in 4.2b from a top view.

suggested that the *grouping* of the elements into bodies should precede the depth analysis. Possibly this consideration is one reason why grouping by motion has been studied as a problem on its own. The Gestaltists, for example, had the notion of "grouping by common fate" which included grouping by common velocity. Potter [1974] used a similar criterion: elements i and j with velocities v_i and v_j respectively are grouped if $|v_i - v_j|$ does not exceed some pre-determined threshold. Gibson [1965] studied the grouping problem sufficiently to become convinced that common velocity is not an adequate grouping criterion, and he subsequently looked for the class of two-dimensional trans-formations that evoke grouping. The two cylinders illustrate the difficulties involved in grouping by motion. Each cylinder contains points spanning a range of velocities, while points having exactly the same speed belong to different objects.

A different explanation for the interpretation of structure

from motion was offered in the original study of the kinetic depth effect [Wallach & O'Connell, 1953] as well as in later studies [Wallach *et al.*, 1956; Jansson & Johansson 1973]. The ability to perceive structure from motion was accounted for in terms of an "effect" produced by lines and contours that change simultaneously in both length and orientation. If only actual lines in the image were considered, the account is manifestly false, since the structure of unconnected dots can be recovered through their motion. Imaginary lines connecting identifiable points were therefore admitted as well [Wallach & O'Connell, 1953]. But the resulting condition (i.e. that the perception of 3-D structure is produced by lines, virtual lines, and contours that change in both length and orientation) is certainly insufficient. Consider for example the random motion of unconnected elements in the frontal plane. The virtual lines between them change constantly in both length and orientation, but no coherent 3-D structure is perceived. The above condition is also necessary in a trivial sense only: the only 2-D transformations of the image that violate Wallach and O'Connell's condition are rigid transformations (of the image, not of the 3-D objects) and uniform scaling. But if the structure of a 3-D object is not recoverable from a single projection, it is not surprising that a uniform displacement, rotation, or scaling of the image itself, are insufficient for revealing the unknown structure.

It has also been conjectured [Wallach & O'Connell, 1953; Borjesson & von Hofsten, 1972] that transformations in which all the elements move along parallel lines in the image are incapable of evoking the kinetic depth effect. But in the two-cylinders display all the elements move parallel to the horizontal axis, yet the 3-D structure is perceptible.

Closely related to the kinetic depth explanation is Gibson's notion of "immediate perception". According to Gibson's theory we are able to correctly interpret changing projections:

"...*not because we have formed associations between optical elements, not even because the brain has organized the optical elements, but because the retinal mosaic is sensitive to transformations as such*" [Gibson, 1957; p. 294].

More generally, in the Gibsonian view perception is constructed from the immediate pairing of stimuli and percepts. There is no need, and no place in the theory for processes that perform inference, interpretation, or computation [Gibson, 1959]. This "immediate perception" approach to vision gives rise to a theory which is opposite, in fundamental aspects, to the computational framework advanced here. The examination of its applicability to the structure-from-motion problem reveals two general shortcomings of the "immediate" approach. The first has to do with the notion of "immediateness". The second concerns the decomposition of object perception into pairings of stimuli and percepts. Let us examine each in turn.

The notion of immediateness: The term "immediate" is relative, in the sense that the qualifications for being immediate depend on the system under consideration. If a system **S** is investigated, then any signal that reaches **S** from the outside can be considered "immediate". For the psychologist, signals of heat or touch produced by peripheral receptors might be thought of as immediate. On the other hand, for the physiologist, who studies for instance the internal mechanisms of Meissner's corpuscle (a touch receptor), the relation between touch and the receptor output cannot be dismissed as immediate. Viewing the relation between the visual input and the perception of structure from motion as immediate does not mean, therefore, that there is not a mediating process involved in this perception. It means, rather, that for the study of the perceptual system the perception of structure from motion can be viewed as an outside agent. Such a view raises two obvious objections. First, the 3-D interpretation requires an explanation, even if for some other process or system it can be viewed as immediate. Second, delimiting the perceptual system in such a way as to make the output of the interpretation process "immediately given" seems questionable.

The decomposition of object perception into stimulus-percept pairs: The computational approach would account for the perception of structure from motion in terms of processes that derive a 3-D representation from the 2-D transformations of the image. The "immediate" approach, on the other hand, explains this perception in terms of "effects" invoked by simple "determinants". In the kinetic depth explanation, for instance, the determinants were lines in the image that change in both length and orientation. The "immediate perception" approach leads to the decomposition of object perception into constituent "effects", since the *true* 3-D structure of an object cannot be viewed as a single effect associated with, for instance, lines changing in length and in orientation. For the interpretation of structure from motion, such percepts as three-dimensionality, rigidity, and coherence, were introduced and associated with various determinants. This decomposition leads to a "perceptual behaviorism" theory of vision, where the Stimulus-Response (S-R) pairs of the behaviorist are replaced by Stimulus-Percept (S-P) pairs. Such a theory accounts for visual perception by compiling a table which pairs stimuli with percepts. Under each stimulus, or class of stimuli, one would find the percepts which this stimulus is capable of eliciting, accompanied perhaps by some potency measure (i.e., how effective the stimulus would be for invoking each percept). This "table" approach seems grossly inUadequate for the S.f.M problem. The perception of a specific structure, such as that of the two cylinders, is far richer than a collection of "effects". That is, in viewing an object in motion, one derives more than "effects" of rigidity, coherence, or three-dimensionality; one perceives the actual shape and motion of the object. It seems to me, therefore, that the proper account for the S.f.M interpretation should be in terms of a process that recovers the correct 3-D structure from 2-D transformations, rather than in terms of a collection of effects associated with specific stimuli.

To investigate the process that derives 3-D structure from the 2-D transformations of the image, we shall follow the general scheme outlined in the introduction and develop a computational theory for the recovery of structure from motion. The problem we shall therefore examine next is how the 3-D structure and motion of objects may be inferred from the 2-D transformations of their projected image.

4.3 Reflective Constraints

The fundamental problem underlying the interpretation of strucuture from motion is the ambiguity of the interpretation. That is, there is no unique structure and motion consistent with a given two-dimensional (2-D) transformation. In the two-cylinders demonstration, for instance, the elements which move on the screen are perceived as elements on 3-D cylinders in rotation, rather than what they actually are, elements undergoing a 2-D translation. Furthermore, the planar and the two-cylinder interpretations are not the only interpretations consistent with the displayed transformation. They are but two of an infinite number of spatial motions of the elements that could produce the same 2-D projection.

To cope with this indeterminacy of structure, the interpretation scheme must incorporate some internal set of constraints that rule out most of the possible 3-D interpretations, and force a unique solution, which in most real cases is also the veridical one. These constraints may also be viewed as a set of *implicit assumptions* about the physical world which, when satisfied, imply the correct solution. Conversely, one can fool the system and create visual illusions by constructing conditions in which the implicit assumptions no longer hold.

Implicit assumptions are required in a variety of perceptual tasks and therefore merit consideration. Their necessity stems from the fact that the relation between objects and appearances is a many-to-one relation.

The visual process can be viewed as being composed of two opposite mappings: visual encoding and visual decoding. In the first, the structure of the visible environment is encoded in a visual message that reaches the eye. This message is then decoded by the visual system to yield the original structure of the environment. The decoding stage is hampered by the fact that many distinct structures may map into the same visual message. In the face of such an inherent ambiguity, perfect decoding becomes impossible. However, in many cases some encodings into a given message are more frequent than others [4.4]. The decoding phase can take advantage of this biased encoding by incorporating biased decoding, or internal constraints, which prefer the most likely interpretation.

Internal constraints are thus viewed as reflecting properties of the physical world which govern the encoding phase. It is in this sense that I called such constraints "reflective". The term will serve to distinguish the reflective constraints that are "utilized" by the visual system, from restrictions imposed upon it, e.g. the locality constraint introduced in Chapter 3.

The reflective role of the internal constraints is made explicit by comparing the reflective constraints with the Gestalt law of *Pragnanz*. This law explains how ambiguous stimuli give rise to specific percepts, by postulating that:

> *"Psychological organization will always be as "good" as the prevailing conditions allow...* [where "goodness"] *...embraces such properties as regularity, symmetry, simplicity, and others"* [Koffka 1935, p. 110].

This general law is further decomposed into a variety of "*Pragnanz* principles" such as the laws of closure, good continuation, good shape, and the law of simplest path. The *Pragnanz* organizational laws are analogous, according to the Gestalt view, to the rules governing mechanical systems. Mechanical systems reach equilibrium through the action of forces. By analogy, in the Gestalt formulation, "stable spatial organizations are held together by an interplay of forces" [*ibid*, p. 439]. The forces are repulsion and attraction in the brain, and the final perceptual structures are those which "reduce the external forces of organization" [*ibid*, p. 171]. The organizational principles are not viewed as related to properties of the external environment, but as peculiarities of the structure of the brain. Consequently, their explanations are cast in terms of physical mechanisms, not in terms of valid constraints on a meaningful computation.

The *Pragnanz* laws were sometimes replaced by postulating that the perceptual system obeys certain minimum principles (e.g. [Attneave, 1972]). It might be noted, however, that minimum principles are only one possible formalism for expressing rules, and that the question of which formalism is preferred is usually of no direct scientific consequence [Feynman, 1965]. For instance, Hamiltonian mechanics, which is based on de Maupertuis' principle of least action, is a minimum principle formulation of Newtonian mechanics. The main question is, therefore, not whether the "organizational" rules of perception are expressible as minimum principles, but what the rules are and what constraints they reflect.

Closer to the notion of reflective constraints is Helmholtz' concept of "Unconscious conclusions" [Helmholtz, 1910] and Gregory's concept of perceptual hypothesis formation [Gregory, 1970]. Like reflective constraints, these notions suggest the application of constraints or assumptions to correctly decode ambiguous stimuli. The main new emphasis of the reflective constraints is in the uniform use of knowledge that reflects general properties of objects, rather than the selective use of knowledge specific to a given object or situation. As stated in Section 3.2, knowledge of the general, 'reflective' kind, is more applicable to the early stages of visual analysis [4.5].

The main requirements of reflective constraints are that they be *restrictive* and *valid.* That is, they should reduce the range of interpretations to (preferably) a unique one, and they should be plausible in the sense that they almost always hold in the environment. Returning to the structure-from-motion interpretation problem, it will therefore be necessary to suggest reflective constraints, and to show that the constraints indeed meet the requirements and hence lead to the correct interpretation.

4.4 The Structure from Motion Interpretation Scheme

Figure 4.3 summarizes the first step in the analysis. We are

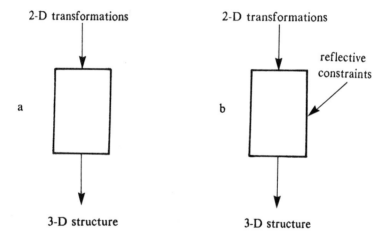

Figure 4.3   The interpretation of structure from motion (4.3a) is driven by two sources: the input transformations, and the reflective constraints (4.3b).

seeking an interpretation process that accepts 2-D projections and recovers the 3-D structure. Since the problem is underdetermined it is advisable to view the process as being driven by two sources: one is the input transformations, the other, the reflective constraints.

The constraint I propose for the interpretation of structure from motion is what I shall call the *rigidity assumption:*

> *Any set of elements undergoing a two-dimensional transformation which has a unique interpretation as a rigid body moving in space should be interpreted as such a body in motion.*

In giving priority to rigid interpretations, I follow several researchers [e.g. Wallach & O'Connell, 1953; Gibson & Gibson, 1957; Green, 1961; Hay, 1966; Johansson, 1975; and a related "three-dimensionality principle" by Johansson, 1964, 1975] who observed that rigidity seems to play a special role in motion perception. However, this "bias for rigidity" is only the starting point of the analysis. The rigidity assumption means that this bias does more than reflect humans' concern with rigid objects. The assumption capitalizes on properties of the physical world in order to arrive at the correct interpretation of under-determined stimuli. The next step in the analysis is therefore to show how the rigidity assumption can be incorporated in an interpretation scheme that will correctly infer structure from motion.

Incorporating the rigidity assumption in an interpretation scheme

To use the rigidity assumption, the interpretation scheme should be able to determine whether a given collection of moving elements has a unique rigid interpretation. The interpretation can then proceed by submitting sub-collections of the elements in the scene to the following *rigidity test:*

> *Does this collection have a unique interpretation as a rigid body moving in space?*

If the answer is negative (either because there is more than a single rigid interpretation or because there are none), then no specific structure is attached to the elements. If the answer is positive, the unique structure discovered is imposed upon the elements.

The rigidity assumption as stated in the previous section requires that the test be administered to small sub-collections of the elements in the scene. This would be necessary if, for example, the scene were composed of several objects participating in different motions. That is, if all the elements in the scene were tested at once for rigidity, the test might fail simply because the elements belong to more than a single object. It follows that the rigidity test must be administered to what I shall term a *nucleus* of elements, namely, a minimal number of elements which is sufficient to determine their structure uniquely. We shall see shortly what this nucleus is.

The above rigidity test raises two immediate problems. The first is whether the test is computable. Namely, is there a procedure for deciding whether a collection of moving elements has a unique rigid interpretation, and for actually determining that structure? The second problem is whether the proposed procedure will result in the correct interpretation of the input projections. As we shall see, the answer to both questions is positive: the test is computable, and the procedure will result in the correct interpretation of the scene. We shall address the second of these problems first, by examining the possible ways in which the interpretation procedure might go wrong.

One possibility for error arises when the rigidity test answers "yes" when it should have answered "no", the second when it answers "no" instead of "yes". The first error involves "false targets": points that actually move independently of each other, yet happen to have a unique interpretation as a rigid body in motion. In this case the interpretation scheme will produce the false structure upon which it has stumbled. The second kind of error results from "phantom structures": points that are the actual projection of a certain moving object, yet are also compatible with the projection of a different object in motion. Because of the additional "phantom structure" the solution would fail to be unique, and consequently no structure would be assigned to the moving elements.

The power of the rigidity-based interpretation scheme stems from the fact that the probabilities of committing a misinterpretation of either type are negligible. We shall examine first the phantom structures problem and show that under simple assumptions they are impossible. That is, given the orthographic projection of a certain object in motion, there is no other object, and no other rigid motion, compatible with the given projection. This claim follows from a theorem concerning rigid objects, which I shall call the *structure from motion theorem:*

> *Given three distinct orthographic views of four non-coplanar points in a rigid configuration, the structure and motion compatible with the three views are uniquely determined.*

This theorem was originally stated and proved by Ullman [1977a, Appendix 1] for five points. Fremlin [1977, personal communication] showed that the requirement can be relaxed to four points. A proof combining [Ullman, 1977a] and [Fremlin, 1977] is given in Appendix 1.

The views in the structure-from-motion theorem are obtained by orthographic projection. As demonstrated, for instance, by the kinetic depth experiments, and by the two-cylinders demonstration, the human visual system can infer structure from orthographic projections; this is the case we shall examine first. In Section 4.5 the results will be extended to cover perspective projections as well.

The theorem has two implications for the interpretation of structure from motion. First, it establishes that 3-D structure can be recovered from as few as four points in three views. This is, then, the minimal nucleus on which the interpretation scheme can operate. Second, the fact that the structure is uniquely determined implies that phantom structures are impossible. Hence, this type of misinterpretation is ruled out.

The second type of misinterpretation mentioned is false targets. It can be shown, however, that in our 3-D world false targets are highly unlikely: the probability that three views of four points not moving rigidly together will admit a rigid interpretation is low. In fact, the probability is zero, provided that the positions of the points are given with complete accuracy. (The argument supporting this claim is statistical, and is given in [Ullman, 1977; Appendix 1].)

Of the two possible misinterpretations listed above, phantom structures are impossible while false targets have zero probability of occurrence. Consequently, the interpretation scheme is virtually immune to misinterpretation. It should be noted that since orthographic projections are employed, the object is determined only up to reflection about the frontal plane. This ambiguity is inherent, since an object rotating by some angle α and its mirror image rotating by $-\alpha$ have the same orthographic projections. Similarly, the absolute distance to the object and its translation in depth cannot be recovered from its orthographic projection. The interpretation in the orthographic case thus allows: a) the decomposition of the scene into objects, b) the recovery of the 3-D structure of these objects up to reflection, and c) the motions of the objects (the relation between the initial and final position and orientation) up to translation in depth.

The formulation of the S.f.M theorem in terms of three distinct views does not imply that the motion of the input image must be discrete (as opposed to continuous). If a continuous motion extends long enough to contain three distinct views (the qualification of "distinct" depends on the accuracy of the interpreting system), then it contains sufficient information for a unique interpretation. The theorem states this mathematical fact without implying how this information should be extracted.

Summary of the main principles: The main principles underlying the structure-from-motion interpretation scheme can be summarized by dividing the interpretation problem into two main components. The first sub-problem is that the 3-D structure and motion are under-determined by the projected 2-D transformations. This difficulty was overcome by incorporating the rigidity assumption as an internal constraint. The second problem in recovering the original motion is that the 2-D transformations in a given scene might be induced by several objects engaged in different 3-D motions. This difficulty was avoided by restricting the interpretation of motion to nuclei of elements which would generally belong to a single object.

Implementation of the scheme and its application to large collections of elements

The proof of the structure-from-motion theorem is constructive, and therefore offers a method for devising a scheme that actually recovers structure from motion. Such a scheme has been implemented at the Artificial Intelligence Laboratory of the Massachusetts Institute of Technology. It is important, however, to maintain the distinction between a general method and a particular algorithm based on this method (see [Marr, 1977a] for a discussion of this distinction). The structure-from-motion scheme can be implemented by various algorithms. For the purpose of the present discussion, the point of interest is the general method. The algorithm, therefore, will not be detailed. Some comments regarding a particular implementation are found in the appendix, however a few conclusions supported by the implementation are worth mentioning here.

Planar objects: The S.f.M theorem guarantees a unique solution for three views of four non-coplanar elements. This does not mean, of course, that the non-coplanarity must be known before the rigidity test is applied. Note also that the non-coplanarity condition is sufficient, but not necessary: four coplanar elements might have many solutions or just a single one, depending on the initial orientation of the planar object and its subsequent rotations in space. If they have a unique solution, the structure will be recovered by the algorithm. Otherwise, the fact that they lie on a single plane will be established, but its orientation and rotation will remain ambiguous. A similar situation arises when the viewed object is composed of only three points. Some three-point configurations are uniquely determined by three views, while others are not. The rigidity-based algorithm can be applied to three views of three points, in which case it is no longer guaranteed to yield a unique solution. However, if the interpretation happens to be unique, it will be discovered by the algorithm.

Number of points vs. accuracy trade-off: In the algorithm, there is a possible trade-off between the number of points (or views) used, and the accuracy required of the input and the computation. If the input data are given with high accuracy, and the computation process is similarly accurate, then four elements are sufficient. A less accurate device (such as, perhaps, the human visual system) might require more elements (or more views) for a reliable and accurate interpretation.

Application to large collections of points: Because real scenes typically contain a large number of elements, the complexity of the computations involved in the interpretation process must be examined. The question is whether the computation remains manageable as the number of elements grows into the hundreds or thousands. The answer is that in realistic scenes the amount of computation required is expected to grow only linearly or approximately linearly with the number of points. Furthermore, most of the process can be carried out in parallel, so that computation time can be largely independent of the number of points.

   To examine the many-elements situation, assume that there are N elements in the image and K objects. We can divide the set of N elements into $N/4$ groups, each containing four neighboring elements, and carry out the interpretation scheme on each of the groups. The computations on the different groups are independent of each other and could be performed in parallel. For all groups interior to the image of an object, namely those in which all four elements belong to the same object, the rigidity test will succeed and the structure will be discovered. The argument now depends on the expectation that the points which comprise a given object will not be distributed randomly over the entire scene. In the case of real, opaque objects, it is expected that each object will have at least one interior group. (The case involving a few transparent objects is somewhat more complex but not unmanageably so, see below.) The first step will thus yield for each of the K objects a set of interior points whose structure and motion are determined, and a set of boundary points which are as yet undetermined. The next step determines, for each of the remaining boundary points, which of the K objects it belongs to. This step can also be executed in parallel for all the points.

The two cylinders and non-opaque objects: The case of non-opaque objects complicates the computation, as points chosen locally can belong to different objects, one behind the other. However, if the number of visible objects at each location is small, the increase in complexity is limited. For example, the S.f.M algorithm has been applied to the two-cylinders display, where two objects are visible, one inside the other. In the central region (where the two cylinders overlap) most of the groups of four points selected at random contain elements of both cylinders and therefore do not have a rigid interpretation. However, 1/8 of the groups do have a rigid interpretation (1/16 for each cylinder). Also, all the groups in the non-overlapping region belong to the bigger cylinder and have a rigid interpretation. Thus, after the first step, over 1/8 of the points are assigned a 3-D structure. A second step completes the interpretation as explained above for boundary points.

The conclusion is that the interpretation scheme can be practicably applied to scenes containing large numbers of elements in motion. Given three views of a scene containing objects in motion, the process would result in the correct interpretation of the scene. The elements will be correctly aggregated into objects, and the 3-D structure of the objects as well as their motion in space will be recovered. This interpretation is accomplished on the basis of the motion alone, without the need for familiarity with the viewed objects, or recognition of the static projections.

4.5 The Perspective Case

The previous section presented an interpretation scheme that accounts for the capacity of the visual system to recover structure from parallel projections. The projection of the environment to the eye, however, is not parallel but *perspective*. Figure 4.4 diagrams schematically the two kinds of projections: a parallel (4.4a) and a perspective projection onto a plane (4.4b).

In this section the interpretation of perspective transformations is examined. Two methods for extending the rigidity-based S.f.M interpretation to perspective projections are considered and compared with human perception: the direct perspective method, and the polar-parallel one. The first handles the perspective case directly and accurately. It is a variation of the parallel S.f.M interpretation scheme modified to reflect the different underlying geometry. That is to say, the interpretation scheme will test 2-D transformations for their compatibility with the perspective projection of a rigid 3-D configuration in motion. The polar-parallel scheme, on the other hand, makes use of the parallel S.f.M method without modifications to yield approximate results to the perspective case. The two methods are collated with human perception. The results suggest that human perception of structure from perspective projections is closer to the polar-parallel scheme than to the direct perspective one. The direct perspective method surpasses human capacity at the price of inherent susceptibility to errors and increasing computational burden. The polar-parallel scheme on the other

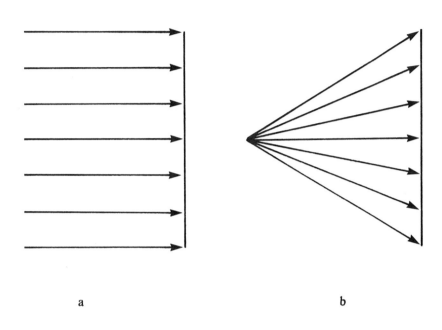

a   b

Figure 4.4 Orthographic projection (4.4a) and perspective projection onto a plane (4.4b).

hand resembles human performance in both its capacity and its limitations. In conclusion, the polar-parallel interpretation scheme is advanced as a competence theory [4.6] for the perception of structure from motion by humans.

4.5.1 The Direct Perspective Scheme

This section examines the direct recovery of structure and motion from perspective projections. An interpretation scheme is outlined, which then serves to establish the following four points:

1. The structure and motion of objects can be recovered from their perspective projections. For the particular scheme used, three views of five elements are usually sufficient for a unique solution.

2. The direct perspective method is inherently susceptible to errors. The reason is that perspective effects are often small, and therefore a procedure that relies on them depends on highly accurate input, and is sensitive to small errors. This problem is especially acute if the interpretation is to be performed locally, since perspective effects diminish with the size of objects. The analysis of the orthographic case revealed that an effective rigidity-based interpretation must be performed locally on nuclei of elements, in order to avoid testing for rigidity elements that do not belong to the same object. The implication is that the direct perspective method is unsuitable for a rigidity-based interpretation of structure from motion.

3. The computation required for the direct perspective interpretation is in general more complex than in the parallel case. However, several types of motion, especially pure translation, are as amenable to direct perspective analysis as they are to the parallel scheme.

4. The perspective interpretation method is qualitatively superior in several aspects to human performance. This superiority does not seem to rely on the particular method used. Rather, it suggests that the capacity to directly interpret changing perspective projections is not incorporated in the human visual system.

The current section is supplemented by Appendix 2 in which an algorithm for perspective interpretation is outlined. At the heart of this algorithm lies a formula called the *polar equation* which performs the interpretation for motions composed of rotations about the vertical axis followed by unrestricted translations. Accordingly, this type of motion will be considered first. The results will then be applied to the more complex situation of unrestricted motion and the simpler case of pure translation.

Rotation about the vertical axis

In Appendix 2 an algorithm is presented that can recover the structure and spatial motion of elements under the following conditions. Two perspective projections of a moving object containing at least four points are given. Between the two frames the object undergoes a rotation about the vertical axis, followed by an arbitrary translation. The first step in the method developed in Appendix 2 is to find α, the angle of rotation. This angle is given by the solution to the polar equation, which has the form:

$$A \sin^2\alpha + B \cos^2\alpha + C \sin\alpha \cos\alpha + D \sin\alpha + E \cos\alpha = 0$$

Although the coefficients A through E are rather complex expressions, they are expressed solely in terms of the projected images, and hence are computable from the two projections. Once the angle α has been found, the 3-D structure and motion can be recovered as well via the formulae listed in Appendix 2. Unlike the parallel case, the solution includes motion in the y direction, i.e. motion *in depth*. The polar equation provides a practical and efficient way of performing the perspective analysis in the special case of rotation about the vertical axis (or any other known axis in the image plane) accompanied by an arbitrary translation.

Unrestricted motion

The algorithm of Appendix 2 for solving the vertical axis case was incorporated in a general scheme which handles unrestricted motion. Instead of a single analytic solution, the general scheme involved the simultaneous solution of a large set of polar equations. The method required a considerable amount of search. Since the angle of rotation is unknown, many axes were examined. The search relied on the assumption that approximate results can be obtained by trying an axis which is sufficiently close in orientation to the true one. There are also alternative methods that avoid the need for a search, and employ instead an iterative procedure to solve a number of simultaneous non-linear equations which relate the rotation, translation, and 3-D coordinates of the elements [4.7]. In any case, the general method was not really practicable, nor was it designed for efficient use. Rather, it served as a vehicle for investigating the perspective case. Rather than developing a S.f.M theorem for the perspective case, use was made of the algorithm to examine the minimum information required for the perspective interpretation. Three views of five points were usually sufficient for the algorithm to recover the correct structure and motion uniquely. In contrast with the orthographic case, two views of five points were often sufficient as well. (For the orthographic case two views of any number of points are insufficient.) In terms of the minimum information required for reliable interpretation, the direct perspective algorithm is thus comparable to the parallel scheme, and, as we shall see, also to the polar-parallel method. It should be noted, however, that these figures hold for the particular algorithm used and depend upon its accuracy. They do not necessarily indicate the absolute minimum required. On the other hand, a less accurate system (as the visual system might be), will require additional views or points for a reliable recovery. When the motion is restricted to pure translation, the direct perspective interpretation is much facilitated, and usually requires less information. We shall examine this case next.

Pure translation

The polar equation can be utilized to construct a simple test that verifies whether the motion of an observed object is composed of pure translation. Substituting $a = 0$ (no rotation) in the polar equation yields $B + E = 0$. The converse is true in a statistical sense: if $B + E = 0$ (for 4 points or more) the elements probably belong to a rigid object in pure translation. If a pure translation has been discovered, the equations in Appendix 2 for computing structure and motion can be used with a set to 0 (see the appendix for details). Thus, pure translation is particularly amenable to direct perspective analysis. It can be tested for, and the translation as well as the 3-D structure are then given by straightforward analytic expressions.

Translation in depth

The sub-case of translatory motion which is directed to or away from the observer has gained special attention in the study of motion perception [Gibson *et al*, 1959; Johansson, 1964; Marmolin, 1973 (I, II); Borjesson & von Hofsten, 1972, 1973; von Hofsten, 1974]. One reason for this special attraction probably stems from the feeling that since the recovery of depth information plays an important part in motion perception, pure motion in depth in some sense epitomizes the interpretation problem. The recovery of motion in depth will be examined here in light of the perspective scheme based on the polar equation. Next, I shall contrast the emerging conclusions with some other theories as well as with experimental data. Two main points will be made. First, the current interpretation scheme can cope successfully with receding and approaching motion. Second, the human visual system is not on par with the perspective interpretation scheme in its ability to infer structure from motion in depth, a fact that strongly suggests that it does not possess the capacity for directly interpreting structure from perspective projections.

For the perspective interpretation scheme, motion in depth is not different from any other translation. If at least four points participate in the motion, the algorithm based on the polar equation would correctly establish the motion as well as the structure. It would first determine whether $B + E = 0$, verifying that the points are engaged in pure translation. Next, the structure and motion in depth would be computed. Note that the procedure verifies that a pure translation has taken place prior to the application of the interpretation formulae. To appreciate the contribution of this preparatory test consider the case of a vertical rod in receding motion. The observed transformation of the rod will be a foreshortening in the vertical dimension, which is also compatible with a *rotation* of the rod in depth (about the horizontal axis). The situation is inherently ambiguous and defies unique interpretation. A study of receding motion by Marmolin [1973] examined the contracting rod situation. (The actual experiments used squares as stimuli, but only one-dimensional changes were considered.) The motion in depth was computed subject to the assumption that the shortening of the rod should be attributed to the receding motion alone. The results were then compared with subjects' judgements. Not surprisingly, there did not exist a good correlation. As Marmolin noted, the observers, faced with the ambiguous stimuli, attributed some of the contraction to motion in depth and some to rotation, thus yielding highly variable results. In contrast with the above scheme, the perspective method would not attribute the changes in object appearance to motion in depth unless it were justified in doing so. Even if the human visual system can recover structure from receding motion, it cannot be expected to achieve a consistent interpretation for the above ambiguous stimuli.

A more revealing experiment would test the perception of structure from motion under conditions which are sufficient to guarantee a unique interpretation. I have carried out such experiments, and the results indicate that humans fail to perceive structure from receding motion under conditions which the perspective interpretation scheme handles with relatively small computational effort. As one example, the two-cylinders display (Section 4.1, Figure 4.1) was tested in receding motion. The presentation comprised eight frames which simulated (when viewed from a distance of 80 cm. from the screen) a gradual motion in depth of two cylinders of diameters 25 and 50 millimeters from an initial distance (of their common axis) of 17 cm. to 62.5 cm. The sequence was run forward (receding motion), backwards (approaching motion), and alternating between both motions in a cycle. The presentation time for each frame was 70 msec., with an ISI of 30 msec. Although the contraction and expansion of the image elicited some impression of motion in depth, the *structure* of the two cylinders could not be recovered from the display. In contrast with this failure, the perspective interpretation scheme, when applied to the projections, could recover the 3-D structure of the two cylinders as well as their displacement in depth.

Both theoretical considerations and experimental observations render the direct perspective method an unlikely candidate for the interpretation of perspective projections. But if the human motion perception system does not incorporate a specialized method for interpreting perspective projections, how are natural scenes, in which the projection is perspective, handled? The answer is that the parallel S.f.M interpretation scheme developed in Section 4.4 might well suffice for the task.

4.5.2 The Polar-Parallel Interpretation Scheme

The parallel S.f.M interpretation scheme can be used almost without modification to yield approximate results in the perspective case as well. Due to the local nature of the computation, reasonable approximations will usually be obtainable. I shall explain what makes this approximation possible and then show how the local operations can be combined into a scheme which is considerably more powerful than each of its components alone.

When an object is sufficiently "far away", its perspective projections can be viewed as slightly distorted orthographic projections. In such a situation, the structure computation used in the orthographic case can be used to provide approximate results in the perspective case as well. The term "far away" means that the difference between the distances from the observer to the points in question is small compared to the distances themselves. That is, if y_i and y_j are the distances of two points from the observer, the points are "far away" if the value of $|y_i - y_j|$ is much smaller than y_i or y_j. Such a condition can hold regardless of the actual distance of the object from the observer, if two requirements are met; (i) the object has densely distributed visible points, and (ii) it is continuous, so that for nearby points in the image, the separation between their spatial sources is also small. In such a case we can take advantage of the inherently local nature of the structure-from-motion computation, i.e. that only four points are needed. If the object in question obeys the above two requirements, then by limiting the field of view to four nearby points at a time, the interpretation is performed on a "far away" object, and therefore the local structure can be recovered. Applications of the orthographic structure-from-motion algorithm to perspective projections showed that it is not very sensitive to distortions, and that it can practicably be used to interpret perspective projections (more quantitative data are given in [Ullman, 1977a]).

Applying the orthographic structure-from-motion scheme locally, and then combining the results, would be different from analyzing the entire image at once as a single orthographic projection. In an orthographic projection there is a single axis of projection common to all of the points. In applying the orthographic scheme to small neighborhoods, while each neighborhood is treated as an orthographic projection, *the axis of projection changes from one neighborhood to another.* To interpret the structure of an object using the orthographic method, we first divide it up into many sub-regions containing about four elements each. We then analyze each region as if it were obtained from an orthographic projection whose axis is along the line from the eye to the center of the region in question. This method for analyzing perspective projections will be called the *polar-parallel* method.

When the local results are combined to form a global interpretation, they give rise to a scheme that surpasses its components in two respects. The first concerns the disambiguation of the true and the reflected 3-D structures. The second concerns the interpretation of receding motion. In the orthographic interpretation the 3-D structure is determined up to a reflection about the image plane, and the rotation is determined up to a sign. These two ambiguities are inherent and coupled, since a rotating 3-D structure has the same orthographic projection as its mirror image rotated by the same amount, but in the opposite direction. The polar-parallel scheme does not share this ambiguity. It can recover both the structure and rotation uniquely. I shall explain how the unique recovery of the structure is performed, and compare the manner by which the direction of rotation is uniquely determined in the polar-parallel scheme to earlier explanations of the same phenomenon, in particular the "motion parallax" cue. Finally, it will be shown that under favorable conditions the interpretation of motion in depth, which eludes the pure parallel interpretation scheme, is also feasible.

Determining the structure uniquely

In orthographic projection the interpretation is determined up to a reflection about the frontal plane. The polar-parallel scheme is not subject to this ambiguity, for although the structure is determined locally only up to a reflection, the requirement for global consistency makes it possible to distinguish between the true and the locally reflected structures. Figure 4.5 helps to illustrate this point. In 4.5a an object O is projected orthographically. The two possible interpretations are depicted: the correct one I (solid line) and the reflected one I' (dotted line). In Figure 4.5b the same object is subjected to a perspective projection. The recovery of the structure is performed locally by the polar-parallel scheme on regions such as O_1 and O_2 in 4.5b. The figure presents the interpretations of two local regions. Each local operation determines the structure up to reflection: I_1 and I'_1 for O_1, and I_2, I'_2 for O_2. Since the direction of the projection changes from O_1 to O_2, the directions of the reflected structures change as well. While I_1 and I_2, the correct interpretations of O_1 and O_2, are parallel to each other, this relation no longer holds for I'_1 and I'_2.

While Figure 4.5 demonstrates the distinction between orthographic and polar-parallel interpretations, it does not reveal how the incorrect structure is ruled out. For all the observer knows, either interpretion in 4.5b might be the true one. The

eous results for about 55% of the time.

The implication of the foregoing analysis is that the motion parallax cue cannot be reliably used independently of an estimation of the rod's orientation [4.8]. To see the advantage of the polar-parallel scheme over the above parallax cue, consider a rotating plane, instead of a rotating rod (to allow the polar-parallel scheme enough points with which to work). If the orientation of the rotating plane is restricted to the 45 degrees section where the nearest points are the slower ones, the "parallax cue" will consistently yield erroneous results, while the polar-parallel scheme will provide the correct answer. There are additional severe problems with using the motion parallax cue: It cannot be used when the rod does not rotate about its midpoint, when the moving elements are not at 180 degrees to each other (i.e. the two points and the axis are not coplanar), or when the rod's motion is not confined to a pure rotation.

Other "cues" proposed for determining the rotation direction are susceptible to the same problems, in particular to the one caused by compound motion. For example, the use of the stagnation points (p and q in Figure 4.6) has been suggested for resolving the rotation ambiguity [Hershberger & Urban, 1970]. Both stagnation points are on the proximal side of the frontal plane, hence when the motion of an element is nullified it might be "declared" as closer than the frontal plane, and this additional information would suffice to resolve the structure and rotation ambiguity. However, like the motion parallax cue, this criterion fails under compound motion situations. The various isolated cues can therefore serve, at best, for an unreliable guess in situations where there is not sufficient information for a recovery by the polar-parallel scheme.

The failure of traditional motion parallax cues under compound motion reflects an important difference between them and the structure-from-motion scheme. Segmentation, structure, rotation, and translation, are not treated independently in the structure-from-motion scheme (unlike [Braunstein, 1962; Gibson 1957; Hay, 1966; Borjesson & von Hofsten, 1972; 1973;

Johansson, 1974; Eriksson, 1974]). If sufficient information (enough points and views) is supplied, the segmentation, structure, rotation, and translation are uniquely determined, although none of them is determined by any "cue" in isolation.

Receding motion

The polar-parallel scheme can be applied to objects in receding motion to determine their structure and motion. As we shall see, the recovery of the structure is more direct and reliable than the recovery of the amount of translation in depth. Figure 4.7 shows an object moving away from an observer. I shall not

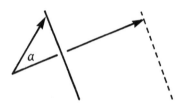

Figure 4.7 Receding motion. As the object recedes, various parts of it rotate with respect to the observer. It would therefore be amenable to polar-parallel interpretation.

analyze this case in detail. It is sufficient to note that while the object as a whole moves in depth, various parts thereof rotate relative to the observer (angle α in Figure 4.7), and hence their structure is recoverable. Consequently, the recovery of the structure and rotation (in the case of receding motion accompanied by rotation) is feasible if the object is large and textured, and if the translation in depth is sufficiently large.

The recovery of the translation in depth is also possible, although it seems that of the various motion parameters, translation in depth is the least amenable to recovery via the polar-parallel scheme.   In the direct perspective method the distortions of the image caused by translation in depth provide a rich source of information that makes this type of motion particularly easy to analyze.   In the polar-parallel scheme, on the other hand, these distortions are viewed as "noise" which impedes the computation and thereby makes receding motion harder to analyze.

A possible method for the recovery of the translation in depth is diagrammed in Figure 4.8. A and B are two elements belonging to a single rigid object O.   The S.f.M scheme recovers the rotation of the object.   Then the rotation can be "undone". That is to say, two new frames are computable from the old ones, such that between them the object would engage only in pure translation [4.9].   After eliminating the rotation, the remaining displacement of the elements is caused by translation alone. The residual translation of A is d_1 (see Figure 4.8).   Since parallel projections are ambiguous with respect to translation along the line of sight, the translation might have an unknown component d_2 along this line (l_1 in the figure).   The discovered translation of B is h_1, possibly accompanied by a component h_2 along the line of sight to B (l_2 in 4.8).   The two known components are sufficient to determine the true motion of the object, even if it is directed away from the observer (i.e along Y in Figure 4.8).   Although the recovery of the motion in depth is possible in principle, it is the most indirect to recover, and the most sensitive to errors of all the parameters of motion.   It is possible (and compatible with existing data) that the perception of receding motion is a somewhat special case, obtained by a measure of the overall contraction of the figure.   It should be noted with respect to this contraction that the receding motion of a 3-D object does not induce a perfectly uniform scaling of its perspective image, i.e. different parts of the object might not contract by exactly the same amount.   However, some measure of

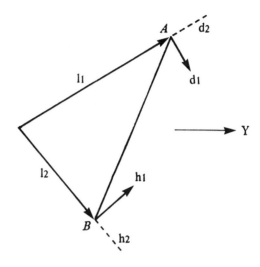

Figure 4.8 The recovery of translation in depth.

the overall contraction can still be adequate for indicating the translation in depth with sufficient accuracy.

4.6 Psychological Relevance

In this section the psychological relevance of the rigidity-based S.f.M scheme will be examined. I shall review various experimental findings that suggest that the principles underlying the polar-parallel system are also used by the human visual system to infer structure from motion. Emphasis will be placed on the following general principles:

(i) The interpretation is performed on the basis of individual, identifiable elements.

(ii) It combines the results of local rigid interpretations applied to nuclei of elements.

(iii) For each local nucleus, the interpretation uses the approximation of orthographic projection.

The need for identifiable elements: The structure-from-motion interpretation scheme helps to explain a phenomenon which Wallach and O'Connell in their original study of the "kinetic depth effect" considered a baffling enigma. When the objects used in their experiments were smoothly curved, so that their shadows did not correspond to identifiable, traceable, 3-D points, the 3-D structure was impossible to recover from the projection:

> *"Curved contours which are deformed without displaying a form feature which identifies a specific point along the curve, are seen as distorting* [rather than moving in depth] ... *This peculiarity is in disagreement with our description of the kinetic depth effect and has delayed our work for years."* [Wallach & O'Connell 1953, p. 209].

Failure to recover structure from motion under these circumstances is to be expected from the structure-from-motion interpretation scheme. According to this scheme the different views are not merely associated somehow into a single whole. Rather, the motion of the individual elements is checked for consistency with the motion of a rigid body. Consequently, the interpretation scheme will fail in the absence of identifiable elements which can be reliably traced throughout the 2-D transformation.

Number of points: A major feature of the structure-from-motion interpretation scheme is that the structure can be recovered from a small number of elements. Four non-coplanar points are always sufficient, and three sometimes suffice, especially if more than three views are provided. For the human visual system the interpretation does not seem to be an all-or-none phenomenon.

The accuracy and stability of the perceived structure increases with the number of elements and views [Green, 1961; Braunstein, 1962]. However the minimum needed for correct interpretation seems to be comparable with the structure-from-motion interpretation scheme: the correct structure of as few as three elements in motion is sometimes perceivable.

Reversals: As explained in the structure-from-motion theorem, the interpretation in the pure orthographic case is determined up to reflection about the frontal plane. The viewed object may thus undergo a depth reversal which must be accompanied by a switch in the observed sense of rotation. Many experiments [e.g., Wallach & O'Connell, 1953; Wallach, O'Connell & Neisser, 1953; White & Mueser 1960], have established that objects viewed in orthographic projection do undergo spontaneous depth reversals accompanied by switches in the observed sense of direction.

Two points in motion: Some cases in which the structure fails to be unique can still be interpreted if additional assumptions are made. The motion of a single line segment (or of its two endpoints) provides an example of such a case. The two points can always be interpreted as the endpoints of a rigid rod whose orientation and rotation are not uniquely determined. However, the two missing variables are related: once the orientation is known the rotation is determined and vice versa. Johansson and Jansson [1968] examined the perception of a single line in motion. Their results concerning the judged orientation of the rod show a tendency to assume that the rod lies in the frontal plane at the moment it has its maximal extension.

Note that this "maximal extension" assumption cannot be a part of the interpretation scheme in general. Consider the two-cylinders example and assume that the total rotation observed is less than 90 degreees. In this case the orientations of pairs of points are inconsistent with the "maximum extension" assumption, and the correct structure, not the one implied by the assumption, is perceived. (Such an experiment was performed by

Wallach & O'Connell [1953]. Rotation through 42 degrees was sufficient to reveal the structure of the hidden objects.) The maximal extension assumption can only serve as a rough and unreliable "last resort" when the general interpretation scheme (which requires uniqueness) fails. Though unreliable in general, this assumption is still the safest one in the impoverished situation of only two elements. It seems that the human visual system tends to use it under such conditions, but without placing much confidence on the results: our 3-D perception of the rotating rod is usually weak and unstable.

Planar objects: Flat objects do not obey the non-planarity requirement, and so the correct recovery of their structure is not guaranteed. Although for most planar objects the structure will nevertheless be recoverable, some cases are inherently ambiguous. For example, let l be the intersection of the object plane with the image plane, and assume that the object rotates about an axis parallel to l. In this configuration the fact that the points are coplanar can be established, but the initial orientation of the plane and its subsequent rotations remain dependent, but unknown variables. Gibson & Gibson [1957] found that planar objects in orthographic projection are indeed ambiguous under the described rotation. (In analogy with the two points case, it seems that in this under-determined situation humans exhibit some tendency to interpret either the initial or the maximal extension position of the plane as frontal.) In contrast with the above condition, the structure of a tilted plane (one that does not pass through the vertical axis) in rotation about the vertical axis is recoverable by the structure-from-motion scheme as well as by human observers.

Absolute and relative depth: The structure-from-motion interpretation scheme recovers the structure of rigid objects. In contrast with the structure which involves relative depth, the absolute depth is not recovered. Furthermore, the relative depth of two objects which move independently of each other cannot be determined. In experiments carried out by Gibson *et al* [1959], subjects were able to determine the correct slant of a projected plane in motion, while the absolute distance estimates varied from three inches to five miles. When several planar objects were presented, their separation in depth was perceivable when they moved rigidly together [Gibson, 1957] but not when their motions were independent [Gibson *et al*, 1959].

Uniqueness of the solution, effects of size, texture, and tilt: It has been mentioned that favorable conditions for the polar-parallel scheme to distinguish between the correct interpretation and its mirror image include large angular extension and dense texture. For planar objects in rotation the unique interpretation is also facilitated when the plane is tilted as already discussed. These expectations are corroborated by findings concerning the Ames trapezoid window [Ames, 1951]. The probability of perceiving the correct orientation and rotation of the window depend on its size, texture, and tilt [Zegers, 1964; Epstein *et al*, 1968; Chapter 5 of this work].

Regarding the unique recovery of the direction of rotation, we have already compared the polar-parallel scheme with the motion parallax cues. Recall also that for the polar-parallel scheme to reliably distinguish between the true and the confusable axes, the object is required to contain enough points at a sufficient angular extension. There are indications [White & Mueser, 1960] that human performance is similar in this respect to the polar-parallel scheme. For a small number of elements the rotation undergoes spontaneous reversals under polar as well as parallel projections.

Few, widely separated points: For the polar-parallel scheme, the recovery of the 3-D structure from the perspective projections of a few (about 4-5) points decreases in accuracy as the perspective effects grow stronger. The perspective effects depend on the ratio between the object's size and its absolute distance from the viewing point. The smaller the perspective effects, the closer the projection is to the orthographic case, and therefore the higher the accuracy of the polar-parallel scheme. In contrast, for a scheme that uses perspective projections directly, large perspective effects should not hinder the interpretation. Braunstein's [1962] findings suggest that the perception of rigidity depends on perspectivity in the expected way. It is strongest for orthographic projection, whereas perspective effects cause perceived distortions in the moving object.

Structure from receding motion: We have seen that for the polar-parallel scheme, receding motion is less amenable to interpretation than, for example, rotation. Favorable conditions for the recovery process include large angular extension and dense texture. It seems that the same requirements must be met for human observers in order to recover structure from receding motion. Gibson *et al* [1959] have shown that the slant of a receding plane can be judged under conditions highly favorable for the polar-parallel scheme. The planar object tested was densely textured and extended 82 degrees of visual angle. The polar-parallel algorithm, when applied to the same receding plane, was also able to recover its structure correctly and uniquely. I have also mentioned that in the receding two-cylinders display (Section 4.5.1), where the conditions were less advantageous from the point of view of the polar-parallel scheme (smaller extension, fewer elements), the recovery of the structure from receding motion proved impossible for human observers, in contrast with rotary motion which does permit interpretation.

Non-rigid motion: The structure-from-motion scheme cannot be applied to non-rigid deformations. However, since the interpretation process is local and requires only a small number of views, it is applicable to quasi-rigid motions which approximate locally and temporarily rigid motion (e.g. "bending" motion, [Jansson & Johansson, 1973]).

CHAPTER 5

THE PERCEPTION OF MOTION FROM STRUCTURE

The previous chapter was devoted to the problem of generating descriptions of 3-D structure and motion from 2-D transformations, where each static view of the scene contains no explicit 3-D information. However, even a single monocular view of a scene often conveys detailed information concerning the 3-D structure of the scene. How such a static interpretation of 3-D structure comes about is of no direct concern here. When such an interpretation does exist it can, however, be utilized in the determination of spatial motion. The current chapter explores issues pertaining to the use of static 3-D perception in the interpretation of visual motion. If the interpretation process discussed in the previous chapter is said to compute structure from motion (S.f.M), the subject of this chapter can be called *motion from structure* (M.f.S), since it uses the known structure to derive spatial motion. Strictly speaking, however, the first method generates descriptions of 3-D structure and motion in space on the basis of 2-D transformations, while the latter infers motion in space from transformations in the interpreted 3-D structure.

Section 5.1 will provide examples illustrating the existence of the motion-from-structure process and some of its properties. The M.f.S scheme requires that the 3-D structure of the scene be perceptible from static views, while the S.f.M scheme can operate regardless of the static 3-D perception. Consequently, when static 3-D perception is present, both schemes might operate simultaneously. Their concurrent operation gives rise to problems of integrating interpretations from different sources. Section 5.2 uses the "Ames illusion" as a framework for discussing various issues concerning the integration of the S.f.M and M.f.S interpretation schemes.

5.1 The M.f.S Interpretation Scheme

The static perception of 3-D structure has an obvious potential for assisting the interpretation of spatial motion. Motion is a continuous change of location and disposition, hence information concerning the 3-D structure of objects, and the way it changes over time, bears directly on the motion of the objects in question. It is not *a priori* clear, however, to what extent static and dynamic interpretations interact. It is conceivable, for example, that they use different internal representations, so that the static 3-D interpretation cannot "write into" the dynamic representation, and cannot affect motion perception, or that static interpretation is too slow to affect motion perception. The current section is aimed at demonstrating that static 3-D interpretation is used in motion perception, and that the static and dynamic interpretations are probably combined into a single representation. To do so, it will not be sufficient to demonstrate that the spatial motion of statically interpretable structures can be perceived. Since the S.f.M scheme can contribute to the perception of motion in space regardless of whether the 3-D structure is statically perceivable, demonstrations in which interpretation by the S.f.M scheme is precluded are required. If the S.f.M scheme is not applicable, but the spatial motion is still appreciable, and is consistent with the changes in the perceived structure, the existence of the M.f.S scheme would be strongly supported.

The demonstrations examined in this section were accordingly designed to disallow S.f.M interpretation by violating various conditions which are essential for a successful application of the S.f.M scheme. The S.f.M scheme can be precluded in a number of ways: by having an insufficient number of points (example 1), an insufficient number of views (example 2), non-rigid motion (examples 3 and 4), or a projection of certain planar objects (such as the Ames window described in Section 5.2). All of these cases can give rise to the perception of continuous motion through 3-D space, provided that the 3-D structure is perceivable from the individual images.

Example 1: Motion of a single line

The first demonstration is diagrammed in Figure 5.1. Segment *l* on the left-hand side of a cube is shown in apparent motion with segment *r* of the same cube. Both segments are visible throughout the presentation. However, in the first frame *l* is bright and *r* is dim, while in the second frame *r* is bright and *l* is dim. When the two frames are shown in alternation, *l* and *r* are seen in apparent motion. The 3-D structure of the cube is perceivable throughout the presentation. When the segment moves from position *l* to *r*, it is seen to move continuously in depth. The trajectory of the line segment is "filled-in" by the visual system, and this filling-in occurs in a 3-D perceptual space. The initial and final positions of the trajectory are determined in this case by the static 3-D interpretation, not by the S.f.M scheme. In contrast with the motion of a line in isolation [Johansson & Jansson, 1968], the position denoted by *l*, at which the line assumes its maximal extension, is not interpreted as lying in the frontal plane. Rather, the perception of the spatial motion is consistent with the static 3-D interpretation of the scene. Furthermore, when the cube reverses in depth, the perceived motion of the line changes accordingly. The perception of spatial motion in this case can be described by saying that the visual system assigns different *3-D labels* to segments *r* and *l* (the term "3-D label" will be used as shorthand for the length and 3-D orientation assigned to a line, or the orientation assigned to a surface, in perceptual space). When the correspondence process identifies the two segments as representing the same entity, the change in their 3-D labels is interpreted as motion in space, the trajectory is filled-in, and the segment is then perceived to move continuously from its initial to its final position.

In conclusion: the static perception of 3-D structure can give rise to the perception of continuous motion through 3-D space. This occurs when the trajectory between elements of different

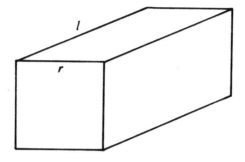

Figure 5.1 Segments *l* and *r* are shown in apparent motion. The static interpretation induces the perception of 3-D motion.

(static) 3-D labels is filled-in by the visual system. The two elements must stand in a correspondence relation for the filling-in to take place and the motion to be perceived. For example, the changes in 3-D labels that occur during Necker cube reversals are not accompanied by a perception of motion.

Some conclusions concerning the representation of visual information

As stated in the introduction, an issue of primary concern to computational vision research is the nature of the internal representation of visual information. We can now summarize some general views that emerge from the study of the correspondence, S.f.M, and M.f.S processes concerning representations related to visual motion. There are indications for the existence of at least two distinct levels of representations, where each level integrates visual information from a variety of sources [c.f. Marr, 1977b]. The first level is a "token space". It is two-dimensional (i.e. depth is not represented at this level), and it supports the correspondence computation. We have seen in Chapter 2 that the tokens in this space can originate from a variety of sources, such as intensity changes in the image, stereo disparity, texture boundaries, and the grouping of other tokens. The second level is a three-dimensional space where static and dynamic interpretations are integrated, and trajectories are filled-in.

The exsistence of these distinct representations might account for the apparent discrepancy between the results reported in Section 2.5, and earlier experiments [Corbin, 1942; Attneave & Block, 1973]. The experiments reported in Section 2.5 probed the affinity metric, which is associated with the token space, and therefore depends on two-dimensional separation. In contrast with Section 2.5 which employed competing motion techniques, the earlier experiments relied on smoothness of motion rating. Smoothness judgements probably depend primarily on the filling-in process, which takes place in the three-dimensional representation space.

Example 2: Motion from two parallel projections

Spatial motion is perceivable from as few as two parallel projections, if both the initial and final 3-D structures are appreciable. When, for instance, line-drawings depicting the parallel projection of a rotating cube are shown in apparent motion, the spatial rotation of the cube is perceivable from two frames. This perception is to be contrasted with the S.f.M interpretation scheme, for which the structure and motion are ambiguous until three distinct views are provided. Thus, the S.f.M scheme cannot be responsible for this interpretation. The observed motion is consistent with the changes in the static 3-D labels assigned to the lines and surfaces in the figures, hence the same process of Example (1) will suffice for performing the interpretation in this case as well.

Example 3: Non-rigid motion

Since the S.f.M scheme seeks rigid interpretations, it is of interest to examine the perception of non-rigid motion. If the initial as well as the final 3-D structures are perceivable from the static images, the motion through space is perceivable even if it involves non-rigid transformations. For example, blocks of various shapes, such as pyramids and cubes, can be shown in alternation in apparent motion. The pyramid can be seen to smoothly transform into the cube, and back into a pyramid. In the course of this deformation different edges move independently of each other, producing a pattern of non-rigid motion which is not recoverable by the S.f.M scheme.

A second example employed various views of a "flag" [Figure 5.2]. The flag could be seen to wave and distort in a non-rigid way. Once again, the distortions of the flag were appreciable from only two views.

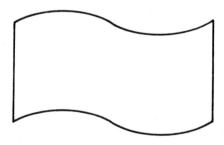

Figure 5.2 The waving flag. Non-rigid distortions of the "flag" are perceptible on the basis of two frames.

Given both the S.f.M and the M.f.S interpretation schemes, non-rigid motion can be interpreted in one of two ways. As mentioned in Chapter 4, if the motion is a local approximation (in both space and time) of a rigid transformation, it can be handled by the S.f.M scheme. Such an interpretation might be applicable, for instance, to the image of a walking person. The person as a whole does not (usually) undergo a rigid transformation, however, when small sub-parts of his body are considered, their motion is approximately rigid. The S.f.M can therefore be applied to recover their structure and motion. Other cases, like the pyramid-cube transformation or the waving flag, cannot be interpreted by the S.f.M scheme, but can be handled by the M.f.S scheme, if both the initial and final 3-D structures are perceptible. If the above two schemes were the only available methods for interpreting non-rigid transformations, then one could predict that non-rigid motions in which the static projections do not give rise to 3-D perception would be incapable of producing a clear and accurate interpretation of structure and motion in space. Some impression of spatial motion may still arise in special cases. In particular, a contraction of the image is liable to induce a sense of receding motion even when the 3-D structure cannot be interpreted (Section 4.5.2).

Example 4: The Mach illusion

The "Mach Illusion" can be demonstrated in the following way. Consider a sheet of paper folded to create a standing v-shaped figure. When viewed monocularly, this shape is ambiguous, the v-shape can reverse in depth [Eden, 1962; Lindsay & Norman, 1972]. An observer views the v-shaped object monocularly, and waits for a depth reversal to occur. The reversal having occurred, he slowly moves his head left and right, up and down, forward and backward. The result is startling: the object seems to move whenever the head does. (Similar illusions can be produced by other constructions, e.g. a wireframe cube.) This illusory motion arises despite the observer's knowledge of the true situation, and it often contradicts shading clues, stability criteria, and touch cues [Eden, 1962]. A relevant point to note is that when the object is close to the eye it appears to distort considerably while it moves; its motion is no longer rigid. Consequently, its illusory motion cannot be attributed to the reversal ambiguity of the S.f.M scheme. If the polar parallel scheme were applied to this configuration, it would discover the correct structure alone; it is immune to Mach's illusion. I expect that humans presented with a "Mach configuration" composed of unconnected elements only, without visible contours, will also be less susceptible to Mach's illusion. Simple reversals might still occur, but the distortions associated with Mach's illusion will disappear.

Additional support for the effect of structure misperception on the misinterpretation of motion will be noted at the beginning of Section 5.2 when the "Ames illusion" is discussed.

When both the S.f.M and the M.f.S schemes are applied to a scene, they usually agree in their results. They will, however, fail to do so when the static perception of structure, which governs the M.f.S process, is erroneous. When such a rivalrous situation occurs, the visual system faces the problem of reconciling conflicting sources of information. There are two main possibilities for resolving such conflicts: compromising on some average solution, or choosing one solution and discarding the other. In fact, when the S.f.M and static 3-D perception conflict, and the difference between them is large, one of them is selected and the other is discarded [5.1]. Consequently, depending on the situation, sometimes one of the processes completely dominates perception, sometimes the other, with possible switches between the two. The Mach illusion mentioned above provides an example where the M.f.S predominates. Wallach, O'Connell, & Neisser [1953], on the other hand, noted examples where the shadow of wireframe objects appeared to have a three-dimensional structure incongruous with the real one. The real structure was usually revealed when the objects were set to motion. In this example, then, the S.f.M process prevailed over the M.f.S.

Another example of rivalry between the processes is given by the extensively studied "Ames window illusion" [Ames, 1951]. The next section examines the Ames illusion and shows that several of its main features are clarified when viewed in light of a rivalry between the two interpretation schemes. The discussion of the Ames illusion is also of interest since it will serve as a framework for bringing together various issues discussed throughout Chapters 4 and 5.

5.2 Ames Phenomena and the Rivalry Between the S.f.M and the M.f.S Interpretation Schemes

An Ames window is a planar trapezoid construction made to appear like a rectangular window in perspective. When the window is rotated, it often appears instead to oscillate back and forth [Ames, 1951]. The illusion is not restricted to Ames' window, as some other figures in rotation are also seen to oscillate while they are actually engaged in a continuous rotation. The possibility of misperceiving the window's direction of rotation is not surprising by itself. It can readily be seen that if segment g in Figure 5.3 is perceived as further away than c, (both, in fact, lie in the frontal plane) then, when the trapezoid rotates around c in *either* direction, the only consistent interpretation is a counter-clockwise rotation (seen from top view). Akin to Mach's illusion, a misjudgement of the structure results in a misperception of the motion.

Unlike Mach's illusion, however, the misperceived structure of Ames' window does not coincide with the reflection of the true structure about the picture plane. If Mach's illusion is presented under parallel projection, the illusion would be explicable without resorting to the M.f.S process, as it becomes merely a case of perceiving the reflected rather than the actual structure. The Ames illusion, on the other hand, can be used to

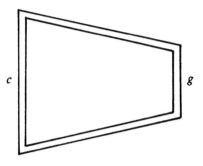

Figure 5.3   A trapezoid window. When such a window rotates about the vertical axis, it is often perceived instead as oscillating back and forth.

demonstrate the effect of the M.f.S process even under parallel projection, since the illusory motion cannot be attributed to the two-way ambiguity inherent in parallel projection.

      Most past discussions of the Ames illusion share the view that its illusory aspect is the result of the structure misperception. Less evident, however, is what causes the illusion to be less than perfect; i.e., what gives away the true disposition of the figure. Under various conditions the illusion is lost, and the veridical rotation is perceived for a large proportion of the viewing time. Binocular vision is one obvious source of veridical information; however, the true structure and rotation are often perceived under monocular viewing as well. Cues of the motion parallax type have been advanced as possible explanations, but for the reasons listed in Section 4.5.2 they can account for the veridical perception only under restricted conditions. The obvious candidate for the correct interpretation is the S.f.M scheme, which is not deceived by structure misperceptions. The

Ames phenomenon can thus be viewed in light of a competition between the two schemes, the M.f.S being responsible for the erroneous interpretation, and the S.f.M providing the correct one. In situations which are unfavorable for the S.f.M scheme the false interpretation is expected to prevail, while under favorable conditions the illusion is expected to decrease in strength [5.2].

In what follows, five phenomena related to the Ames illusion will be examined under three viewing categories. Predictions concerning these phenomena will be made, and compared with empirical data whenever possible. The three viewing categories are:

1. A vertical plane in parallel projection.
2. A tilted plane in parallel projection.
3. A vertical plane in perspective projection.

A "vertical plane" means that the window-plane passes through the vertical axis, and the window rotates about this axis. This is an instance of a configuration which is ambiguous to the parallel S.f.M scheme. A "tilted plane" is a non-frontal plane that passes through the horizontal X-axis but rotates about the vertical Z-axis. The structure of such a plane is recoverable by the parallel S.f.M scheme (Section 4.2.5, sub-section on planar objects).

These three viewing categories differ in several respects that are relevant to the subsequent discussion. The main difference is in the applicability of the parallel and polar-parallel S.f.M schemes. In category (1), both schemes are inoperative. Category (2) is amenable to the parallel scheme only, and category (3) is amenable to the polar-parallel scheme. I shall examine below in more detail the applicability of the S.f.M and the M.f.S schemes to the different categories. These differences will then be used in the analysis of the Ames-related phenomena.

The parallel S.f.M interpretation scheme is applicable to the second category, and the polar-parallel to the third. In the first category neither the parallel nor the polar-parallel scheme is applicable. Consequently, in category (1) the M.f.S is expected to prevail. The failure of the parallel S.f.M scheme depends on the object being planar: non-planar objects are similar to category (2). That is, they are expected to be recoverable by the S.f.M scheme up to a reflection ambiguity. The second category is amenable to the parallel S.f.M interpretation, but since the polar-parallel scheme is inapplicable, the structure can be determined only up to a reflection. In the third category the structure can be recovered *uniquely* by the polar-parallel S.f.M scheme. Increases in angular extension, tilt, and texture (density of feature points) help the S.f.M scheme and therefore their effect on the various phenomena can be predicted. The predictions will be qualitative in nature, since some secondary effects are ignored [5.3], and since the relative strength of the two interpretation schemes can be compared only in qualitative terms.

Analysis of five Ames-related phenomena

The list of phenomena discussed below include reversals, preferred points of reversals, preferred orientation range, preferred sense of rotation, and the recovery of the correct orientation. We will discuss each in turn.

Phenomenon 1: Reversals of the rotation direction

Some misconceptions regarding the Ames illusion stemmed from examining the occurrence of reversals independent of other phenomena. Ames' explanation of his illusion in terms of misperceived structure had been challenged [Power and Day, 1973] on the grounds that figures whose structure is not misperceived are also subject to spontaneous perceptual reversals in their direction of rotation (especially when the viewing conditions approximate a parallel projection). As we have seen in the discussion of the S.f.M problem, the structure and motion of *any* object are determined by its parallel projections only up to a reflection and are therefore susceptible to spontaneous reversals of both the structure and the sense of rotation. Unlike the spontaneous reversals that characterize parallel projection, those caused in the Ames illusion by structure misperception are expected to occur at particular orientations, namely when the rotating window passes through the frontal plane. A second distinction between the two reversals is that only the spontaneous ones are accompanied by reversals of the structure. *The mere occurrence of reversals should not be confused with Ames' illusion*, and the confusion is avoided if other phenomena, such as preference for points of reversal, are examined as well. In the absence of structural misperception, (1) and (2) of the three categories listed above are expected to exhibit spontaneous reversals, even if non-planar objects are employed [Wallach & O'Connell, 1953]. Category (3) should be relatively immune to such reversals, especially when the viewed object is large and has densely distributed feature points [Gibson *et al*, 1959]. Little can be said about the *rate* of reversals, although this is one of the frequently tested parameters. The reason is that the frequency of spontaneous reversals under parallel projection cannot be predicted, as it depends on unknown parameters of the visual system and not only on the stimuli under consideration. It can be expected, however, that when the M.f.S prevails completely, as in category (1), the rate of reversals will approach two per cycle. Experimental work [Epstein *et al*, 1968; Cross & Cross, 1969] has established that the frequency of spontaneous S.f.M reversals is smaller: under the experimental conditions it was on the order of 0.5 per cycle. Since the rate of reversals induced by the M.f.S is considerably higher, it is expected that the frequency of reversals will increase as the S.f.M interpretation decreases in strength compared to that of the M.f.S scheme. The frequency should be highest in category (1) and lowest in (3), and decrease with the object's size, texture and tilt. These expectations are in agreement with experimental data [Zegers, 1964; Epstein *et al*, 1968].

Phenomenon 2: Preferred points of reversal

In category (1) reversals are expected to occur whenever the object passes through the frontal plane. In category (2) the

number of such reversals might decrease, with a possible introduction of spontaneous reversals at other orientations. Category
(3) might, in addition, exhibit some reversals at arbitrary
positions caused by switches from one mode of interpretation to
the other. Unlike category (2) these spontaneous switches would
be accompanied by a change in the perceived structure which is
not necessarily a reflection about the picture plane. There are,
then, three distinct types of reversal in the perceived direction of
rotation.

(a) Spontaneous reversals associated with parallel projections.
They occur at non-specific points and are accompanied by
structural reversals. They are expected to occur most
frequently in category (2).

(b) Reversals due to the misperceived structure, occuring at
particular points, and not accompanied by structural reversals.
They are expected to occur most frequently in category (1).

(c) Reversals caused by transitions from one interpretation
dominance to another. These are accompanied by structural
changes, but not necessarily reversals. They are expected to
occur primarily in category (3), are possible in (2), and impossible in (1).

These distinctions remain as predictions for future research, since
the structural changes associated with the reversals have not been
examined.

Phenomenon 3: Preferred range of orientation

In category (1) the object's orientation is expected to be
confined to a sector determined primarily by the perceived
structure. If, for instance, the frontal trapezoid window is
perceived instead as a rectangle rotated by 45 degrees from the
frontal plane, it is expected to be seen as oscillating between
orientations of about +45 and -45 degrees, thereby covering a
sector of 90 degrees. If, on the other hand, the veridical motion
is always perceived, there would be no preferred range of

orientation, and the object would be seen to cover the entire range of 360 degrees. In category (2) the orientation range is expected to be wider than in (1) since the S.f.M supplies veridical orientation information. These predictions are supported by [Olson, 1974]. It is conceivable that of the two orientations compatible with the parallel projection, the one congruent with the static structure will be preferred. As a result, in category (2) one sector of 180 degrees will be consistently preferred over the other. Category (3) should show less preference for a particular sector, especially if the window is large, textured, and tilted.

Phenomenon 4: Preferred sense of rotation

The M.f.S interpretation scheme would give rise to oscillatory motion in which no sense of rotation would be preferred. The parallel S.f.M as well does not have any inherent bias for a particular rotation. Although the type of motion is different in categories (1) and (2) (more oscillations in (1)), no preference for rotation-direction is therefore expected in either category, as well as in parallel projection in general. Category (3) on the other hand, should exhibit a preference for the actual direction of rotation, since the polar-parallel scheme is capable of recovering the true rotation unambiguously.

Phenomenon 5: Seeing the correct orientation

In category (1), the correct orientation cannot be recovered at all. In category (2) the perceived orientation is expected to be, on the average, closer to the actual one *or* to its reflection about the picture plane. Only in category (3) can the orientation be recovered correctly and unambiguously. These conclusions are supported by experimental data [Gibson *et al*, 1959; Wallach & O'Connell, 1959].

In summary, the Ames-related phenomena can be attributed to the rivalry between the S.f.M and M.f.S schemes, and they are governed by the following three principles.

1. The misperceived structure gives rise, through the M.f.S scheme, to illusory judgments of the structure and rotation.

2. The polar-parallel scheme is the source of the veridical perception.

3. In cases that approximate parallel projection the polar-parallel scheme degenerates to the pure parallel scheme, which can supply correct information only up to a reflection about the frontal plane.

EPILOGUE

Some of the essential capacities underlying the interpretation of visual motion are epitomized by the three types of relations that the visual system can establish between pairs of stimuli. The first type is the *replacement* relation. One figure might be perceived as disappearing and being replaced by a subsequent one, (like a face replacing an obstacle in a peekaboo game). The second type is the *transformation* relation. One figure might be seen as changing into another, without ever losing its identity, such as the frog transforming into a prince in an animated movie. The third type is a *motion* relation, where different views are perceived as representing the same, unchanging, object in motion.

It seems appropriate to conclude this work by accounting for these fundamental relations in terms of the correspondence and the interpretation processes.

Depending on the affinity and spatio-temporal relations between their constituents, a pair of stimuli shown in succession may or may not be matched by the correspondence process. The situations where they fail to correspond give rise to the replacement relation. For two corresponding stimuli, the interpretation process can make the distinction between a change of structure and a motion relation. If the transforming scene can be interpreted as a rigid object in motion, it will be appreciated as such. Otherwise, a change is indicated.

APPENDIX 1

THE STRUCTURE FROM MOTION THEOREM

The structure from motion theorem:

> Given three distinct orthographic projections of four non-coplanar points in a rigid configuration, the structure and motion compatible with the three views are uniquely determined up to a reflection about the image plane.

Comment: It is assumed that a correspondence between the projections has already been established. Namely it is known which points in the three views are the projection of the same source point in space.

Nomenclature: Let O, A, B, and C be the four points. The motion of the object is composed of translation and rotation. In orthographic projection the recovery of the translation in depth is impossible, and the recovery of the remaining translation component is trivial, since it is congruent in space and in the image plane. It is also assumed that corresponding points (i.e. the three projections of the same 3-D point) have been identified. The problem is therefore equivalent to the following formulation. The orthographic projections of the four points on three distinct planes $\Pi 1$, $\Pi 2$, $\Pi 3$, are given, and the 3-D configuration of the points is to be reconstructed. We choose a fixed coordinate system with its origin at O. Let $\underline{a}$, $\underline{b}$, and $\underline{c}$ be the vectors from O to A, B, and C, respectively. Let each view have a 2-D coordinate system (p_i, q_i), with the image of O at its origin. That is, $\underline{p}_i$ and $\underline{q}_i$ are orthogonal unit vectors on Πi. Let the coordinates of (A, B, C) on Πi (the image coordinates) be $(x_{ai}\, y_{ai},\, x_{bi}\, y_{bi},\, x_{ci}\, y_{ci})$ for $i = 1,2,3$. Finally, let $\underline{u}_{ij}$ be a unit vector along the intersection line of Πi and Πj.

The image coordinates are given by:

$$\text{(1)}$$

$$
\begin{aligned}
x_{ai} &= \underline{a}\,\underline{p}_i & y_{ai} &= \underline{a}\,\underline{q}_i \\
x_{bi} &= \underline{b}\,\underline{p}_i & y_{bi} &= \underline{b}\,\underline{q}_i \\
x_{ci} &= \underline{c}\,\underline{p}_i & y_{ci} &= \underline{c}\,\underline{q}_i
\end{aligned}
$$

The unit vector $\underline{u}_{ij}$ lies on Πi which is spanned by $(\underline{p}_i, \underline{q}_i)$ hence:

$$u_{ij} = \alpha_{ij}\underline{p}_i + \beta_{ij}\underline{q}_i, \qquad \alpha_{ij}^2 + \beta_{ij}^2 = 1 \tag{2}$$

The unit vector $\underline{u}_{ij}$ is also on Πj which is spanned by $(\underline{p}_j, \underline{q}_j)$ hence:

$$u_{ij} = \gamma_{ij}\underline{p}_j + \delta_{ij}\underline{q}_j, \qquad \gamma_{ij}^2 + \delta_{ij}^2 = 1 \tag{3}$$

From (2) and (3) we obtain the vector equation:

$$\alpha_{ij}\underline{p}_i + \beta_{ij}\underline{q}_i = \gamma_{ij}\underline{p}_j + \delta_{ij}\underline{q}_j \tag{4}$$

Taking the scalar product of (4) with $\underline{a}$, $\underline{b}$, and $\underline{c}$ respectively, we get:

$$\text{(5)}$$

$$
\begin{aligned}
\alpha_{ij}\,x_{ai} + \beta_{ij}\,y_{ai} &= \gamma_{ij}\,x_{aj} + \delta_{ij}\,y_{aj} \\
\alpha_{ij}\,x_{bi} + \beta_{ij}\,y_{bi} &= \gamma_{ij}\,x_{bj} + \delta_{ij}\,y_{bj} \\
\alpha_{ij}\,x_{ci} + \beta_{ij}\,y_{ci} &= \gamma_{ij}\,x_{cj} + \delta_{ij}\,y_{cj}
\end{aligned}
$$

These three equations in $(\alpha_{ij}, \beta_{ij}, \gamma_{ij}, \delta_{ij})$ are linearly independent. To see this, assume that there exist three scalars η, λ and μ, such that:

$$\text{(6)}$$

$$
\begin{aligned}
\eta \underline{p}_i\,\underline{a} + \lambda \underline{p}_i\,\underline{b} + \mu \underline{p}_i\,\underline{c} &= 0 \\
\eta \underline{q}_i\,\underline{a} + \lambda \underline{q}_i\,\underline{b} + \mu \underline{q}_i\,\underline{c} &= 0 \\
\eta \underline{p}_j\,\underline{a} + \lambda \underline{p}_j\,\underline{b} + \mu \underline{p}_j\,\underline{c} &= 0 \\
\eta \underline{q}_j\,\underline{a} + \lambda \underline{q}_j\,\underline{b} + \mu \underline{q}_j\,\underline{c} &= 0
\end{aligned}
$$

In this case the vector $\underline{\theta} = (\eta\underline{a} + \lambda\underline{b} + \mu\underline{c})$ would be orthogonal to all of $\underline{p}_i$, $\underline{p}_j$, $\underline{q}_i$, and $\underline{q}_j$. Since Πi and Πj are distinct, this implies that $\underline{\theta} = \underline{0}$. But since (O, A, B, C) are non coplanar, $\underline{\theta} = \eta\underline{a} + \lambda\underline{b} + \mu\underline{c} = \underline{0}$ implies that $\eta = \lambda = \mu = 0$, hence the equations are linearly independent.

Combined with the requirement $\alpha_{ij}^2 + \beta_{ij}^2 = \gamma_{ij}^2 + \delta_{ij}^2 = 1$, equations (5) have two solutions of the same absolute value but opposite sign. Choosing one of these solutions, we have found (up to a sign) the vectors $\underline{u}_{ij}$ in terms of $(\underline{p}_i, \underline{q}_i)$ and $(\underline{p}_j, \underline{q}_j)$. We can next determine the distances:

(7)

$$d_1 = \| \underline{u}_{12} - \underline{u}_{13} \|$$
$$d_2 = \| \underline{u}_{12} - \underline{u}_{23} \|$$
$$d_3 = \| \underline{u}_{13} - \underline{u}_{23} \|$$

We now examine the triangle whose sides are d_1, d_2, d_3. If there is a solution to the reconstruction problem, then there exists at least one such triangle. It might, however, be degenerate, i.e. at least one of the distances equals zero. In the non-degenerate case the triangle is unique, and all its vertices are known to lie at a unit distance from the origin. The three vertices and the origin thus define two possible tetrahedra, one being the reflection of the other. For each tetrahedron, the projections of A, B, and C on the three planes are known, and they determine a unique 3-D configuration.

The degenerate case: If one of the distances $d_i = 0$ ($i = 1,2,3$), then all are, and the tetrahedron degenerates to a single line. Otherwise, two of the planes Π_i ($i = 1,2,3$) would coincide, contrary to the assumption. To prove the degenerate case we shall first establish two lemmas.

Let $p_1 = (x_1\ y_1)$, $p_2 = (x_2\ y_2)$, $q_1 = (x'_1\ y'_1)$, $q_2 = (x'_2\ y'_2)$ be four points in a plane $(x\ y)$ such that $(q_1\ q_2)$ is not the reflection of $(p_1\ p_2)$ about the y-axis, and suppose that the lines $p_1 - q_1$ and $p_2 - q_2$ (which we shall call "trajectories") are parallel to the x-axis. The pair $q_1 - q_2$ is now rotated by α about the origin O. Let $q'_1 = (u_1\ v_1)$ and $q'_2 = (u_2\ v_2)$ be the rotated pair. O, p_1, and p_2, are assumed to be non-collinear.

Lemma 1: There exists exactly one angle $\alpha > 0$ such that the lines $p_1 - q'_1$ and $p_2 - q'_2$ are parallel.
Proof: For $i = 1,2$:

(8)

$$u_i = x'_i \cos\alpha - z'_i \sin\alpha,$$
$$v_i = x'_i \sin\alpha + z'_i \cos\alpha$$

If, following the rotation, the lines are parallel, then their slopes coincide, namely:

(9)

$$\frac{y_1 - v_1}{x_1 - u_1} = \frac{y_2 - v_2}{x_2 - u_2}$$

(There is also the possibility that the two lines are parallel to the y-axis in which case the denominators in both the above expressions vanish. We shall see, however, that in this case the solution is still unique.)

Substituting for v and w using (8) yields: ($y'_1 = y_1$ and $y'_2 = y_2$)

(10)

$$\frac{y_1 - x'_1 \sin\alpha - y_1 \cos\alpha}{x_1 - x'_1 \cos\alpha + y_1 \sin\alpha} = \frac{y_2 - x'_2 \sin\alpha - y_2 \cos\alpha}{x_2 - x'_2 \cos\alpha + y_2 \sin\alpha}$$

Which reduces to the form:

(11)

$$a \sin\alpha + b \cos\alpha = b$$

where:

$$a = x_1 x'_2 - x'_1 x_2$$
$$b = x_1 y_2 + x'_1 y_2 - y_1 x_2 - y_1 x'_2$$

Given a and b this equation has exactly one solution for α, given by:

(12)

$$\sin\alpha = 2ab / (a^2 + b^2)$$
$$\cos\alpha = (b^2 - a^2) / (a^2 + b^2)$$

The only case where there is no unique solution to (12) is when both a and b are equal to 0. In this case (11) provides two equations in x'_1 and x'_2. If the equations are independent, then their solution is: $x'_1 = -x_1$, $x'_2 = -x_2$ namely, (q_1 q_2) is the reflection of (p_1 p_2) about the y-axis, contrary to the assumption. If they are independent then $x_1/x_2 = y_1/y_2 = x'_1/x'_2$ which violates the non-colinearity assumption. If there exists a rotation β which makes the denominators in (9) equal to zero, this β is still a solution -- and the only solution -- to equation (11). ∎

Lemma 2: If the projections of two objects O and O' on the frontal plane coincide, and if the coincidence is maintained after both objects rotate by the same amount ψ (ψ < 180 degrees) about the vertical axis, then O and O' are congruent.
The proof is straightforward and will be omitted.

We wish to establish the uniqueness of the interpretation for (O, A, B, C) rotating about a fixed axis. Let the rotation axis be the z-axis of a coordinate system whose origin is at O, and let y-z be the image plane. Let Ω be the object (O, A, B, C). If the interpretation is not unique then an object $\Omega' = $ (O, A', B', C') exists whose rotations are different than those of Ω, but the three projections of Ω and Ω' coincide. (By lemma 2, if the rotations are the same the objects are congruent.)
Between the first and second views, Ω is rotated by some angle $\alpha_1 \neq 0$, and Ω' by β_1. Between the second and third views, Ω is rotated by $\alpha_2 \neq 0$, Ω' by β_2. Throughout the rotations the projections of Ω and Ω' on the image plane y-z coincide. Let $p_1 = (x_1 \ y_1)$ be the projection of A on the x-y plane, $p_2 = (x_2 \ y_2)$ the projection of B, $q_1 = (x'_1 \ y'_1)$ the projection of A', and $q_2 = (x'_2 \ y'_2)$ the projection of B'. Without loss of generality (p_1, p_2) and (q_1, q_2) satisfy the requirements of Lemma 1 (since two such pairs must exist, if not the projections of A, B, A', B', then the projections of A, C, A', C').
Claim: $\alpha_2 = \beta_2$
Proof of the claim: Between the first and second view Ω (and so $p_1 \ p_2$) is rotated by α_1 and Ω' (and so $q_1 \ q_2$) is rotated by β_1, and the resulting trajectories $p_1 - q_1$ and $p_2 - q_2$ remain parallel to the x-axis. If Ω did not rotate, and Ω' rotated by $\beta_1 - \alpha_1$, then the trajectories would still be parallel to each other (though

not to the x-axis). According to lemma 1 there is a unique angle for which this will happen. Call this angle ψ, then $\beta_1 - \alpha_1 = \psi$. Between the first and third view Ω rotated by $\alpha_1 + \alpha_2$ and Ω' by $\beta_1 + \beta_2$ resulting once again in parallel trajectories. From the uniqueness of ψ, we get: $(\beta_1 + \beta_2) - (\alpha_1 + \alpha_2) = \psi$.

But since:

$$\beta_1 - \alpha_1 = \psi, \qquad \beta_2 = \alpha_2.$$

Between the second and third view the two objects retain their coincidence of projection through a common rotation. According to lemma 2 they are congruent. ∎

The above proof offers a method for actually computing 3-D structure from three orthographic projections. The computation must be expressed in terms of the measurable parameters, which are the 2-D coordinates of the four points in the three views expressed in terms of (p_i, q_i) for $i = 1,2,3$. Equations (5) use these parameters to determine u_{ij}, the unit vectors generating the tetrahedron. If the tetrahedron is non-degenerate, two views are sufficient to determine the 3-D configuration. The 3-D position of a point can be found by the intersection of the perpendiculars to its projections on two planes. The recovery of the structure in the degenerate case is not given by the proof but can be determined by straightforward trigonometric considerations [Ullman 1977a Appendix 2]. Other algorithms, that satisfy better the requirement for biological feasibility (Section 3.3), also exist, but they will not be discussed here.

APPENDIX 2

STRUCTURE FROM PERSPECTIVE PROJECTIONS

The problem addressed in this appendix is the computation of structure and motion from perspective projections. Two "snapshots" depicting perspective views of a rigid object in motion are given. The object is composed of a number of identifiable feature points. It is assumed that the correspondence between the two frames is already known.

It should be noted that the structure and translation can be determined from the views only up to a single scaling factor. There is no way of telling whether the object is "small and nearby" or "big but far away". To put it more precisely, let O be an object (namely, a collection of 3-D coordinates x_i, y_i, z_i) which undergoes a rigid transformation R + T, where R denotes a rotation and T a translation-vector. The perspective projections of this object in motion are indistinguishable from those of an object cO (namely, the collection of 3-D coordinates cx_i, cy_i, cz_i) undergoing a transformation R + cT.

In the first part of this appendix the motion of the observed object is restricted to combinations of rotations about the vertical axis and arbitrary translations. Next, the case of pure translation is examined. The main novelty of this appendix is in the reduction of these cases to the solution of a single equation, which is explicitly given. The case of unrestricted motion will not be discussed. For further discussion of the subject see [Ullman, 1977a; Appendix 3].

The vertical rotation case

The structure and motion are recovered by operating on three points at a time. Let the 3 points be $(x_1\ y_1\ z_1)$, $(x_2\ y_2\ z_2)$ and $(x_3\ y_3\ z_3)$. All three points undergo a common rigid transformation R + T, where R is a rotation by θ degrees about the vertical Z-axis, and T is a translation vector $(\Delta x\ \Delta y\ \Delta z)$. If

$(x_i'\ y_i'\ z_i')$ are the coordinates of the i'th point following the transformation, then:

(1)

$$x_i' = x_i \cos\theta - y_i \sin\theta + \Delta x$$
$$y_i' = x_i \sin\theta + y_i \sin\theta + \Delta y$$
$$z_i' = z_i + \Delta z$$

while the coordinates $(x_i\ y_i\ z_i)$ are not recoverable from the image, the angles $\phi_i = x_i/y_i$ (yaw angle) and $\eta_i = z_i/y_i$ (pitch) are. Following the rigid transformation the yaw angle is:

(2)

$$\phi_i' = x_i'/y_i' = \frac{x_i \cos\theta - y_i \sin\theta + \Delta x}{x_i \sin\theta + y_i \cos\theta + \Delta y}$$

and the pitch angle is:

$$\eta_i' = z_i'/y_i' = \frac{z_i + \Delta z}{x_i \sin\theta + y_i \cos\theta + \Delta y}$$

x_i and z_i can be eliminated from (2) by substituting $x_i = \phi_i\ y_i$ and $z_i = \eta_i\ y_i$. Seven unknown parameters thus remain: y_1, y_2, y_3 (the structure), and θ, Δx, Δy and Δz (the motion). since the interpretation is determined up to a single scaling factor, there are actually only 6 unknowns to recover and 6 (non linear) equations: 3 for the yaw and 3 for the pitch. An elaborate process of substitutions transforms the 6 equations into a single equation in θ alone. The equation has the form:

(3)

$$\alpha_3\beta_1\beta_2\ (\phi_1' - \phi_2') + \alpha_2\beta_1\beta_3\ (\phi_3' - \phi_1') + \alpha_1\beta_2\beta_3\ (\phi_2' - \phi_3')$$
$$=$$
$$\alpha_1\alpha_2\beta_3\ (\eta_2' - \eta_1') + \alpha_1\alpha_3\beta_2\ (\eta_1' - \eta_3') + \alpha_2\alpha_3\beta_1\ (\eta_3' - \eta_2')$$

where:

$$\alpha_i = \phi_i'\ \phi_i \sin\theta + \phi_i' \cos\theta + \phi_i \cos\theta + \sin\theta$$

and:

$$\beta_i = \eta_i' \; \phi_i \sin\theta + \eta_i' \cos\theta - \eta_i$$

After numerous steps of multiplication, collection of terms, and simplification, equation (3) assumes the form:

$$\text{(4)}$$

$$A \sin^2\theta + B \cos^2\theta + C \cos\theta \sin\theta + D \sin\theta + E \cos\theta = 0$$

Equation (4) will be called the *polar equation.*

The next few pages list the coefficients A, B, C, D, and E. The terms are rather complex, however they are expressed entirely in terms of the measurable quantities ϕ_i and η_i. Some simplification of the terms can be gained by an appropriate choice of the coordinate system, e.g. choosing the Y-axis so that $\phi_1 = \eta_1 = 0$.

A, the coefficient of $\sin^2\theta$

$(\; (1 + \phi_1 \; \phi_1') \; \eta_2' \; \eta_3 \; (1 + \phi_2 \; \phi_3') \;) -$
$(\; (1 + \phi_1 \; \phi_1') \; \eta_2 \; \eta_3' \; (1 + \phi_2' \; \phi_3) \;) +$
$(\; (1 + \phi_2 \; \phi_2') \; \eta_1 \; \eta_3' \; (1 + \phi_1' \; \phi_3) \;) -$
$(\; (1 + \phi_2 \; \phi_2') \; \eta_1' \; \eta_3 \; (1 + \phi_1 \; \phi_3') \;) +$
$(\; (1 + \phi_3 \; \phi_3') \; \eta_1' \; \eta_2 \; (1 + \phi_1 \; \phi_2') \;) -$
$(\; (1 + \phi_3 \; \phi_3') \; \eta_1 \; \eta_2' \; (1 + \phi_1' \; \phi_2) \;)$

B, the coefficient of $\cos^2\theta$

$(\; \eta_2' \; \eta_3 \; (\phi_1' - \phi_1) \; (\phi_3' - \phi_2) \;) +$
$(\; \eta_2 \; \eta_3' \; (\phi_1' - \phi_1) \; (\phi_3 - \phi_2') \;) +$
$(\; \eta_1 \; \eta_3' \; (\phi_2' - \phi_2) \; (\phi_1' - \phi_3) \;) +$
$(\; \eta_1' \; \eta_3 \; (\phi_2' - \phi_2) \; (\phi_1 - \phi_3') \;) +$
$(\; \eta_1' \; \eta_2 \; (\phi_3' - \phi_3) \; (\phi_2' - \phi_1) \;) +$
$(\; \eta_1 \; \eta_2' \; (\phi_3' - \phi_3) \; (\phi_2 - \phi_1') \;)$

C, the coefficient of $\cos\theta * \sin\theta$

$(\eta_2' \ \phi_1' \ \phi_2 \ \phi_3' \ (\eta_3 - \eta_1) \ ) +$
$(\eta_1' \ \phi_1 \ \phi_2' \ \phi_3' \ (\eta_2 - \eta_3) \ ) +$
$(\eta_3' \ \phi_1' \ \phi_2' \ \phi_3 \ (\eta_1 - \eta_2) \ ) +$
$(\eta_1 \ \phi_1' \ \phi_2 \ \phi_3 \ (\eta_2' - \eta_3') \ ) +$
$(\eta_2 \ \phi_1 \ \phi_2' \ \phi_3 \ (\eta_3' - \eta_1') \ ) +$
$(\eta_3 \ \phi_1 \ \phi_2 \ \phi_3' \ (\eta_1' - \eta_2') \ ) +$
$(\eta_1 \ \eta_2' \ (\phi_2 - \phi_1') \ (1 + \phi_3 \ \phi_3')) +$
$(\eta_1' \ \eta_2 \ (\phi_2' - \phi_1) \ (1 + \phi_3 \ \phi_3')) +$
$(\eta_1' \ \eta_3 \ (\phi_1 - \phi_3') \ (1 + \phi_2 \ \phi_2')) +$
$(\eta_1 \ \eta_3' \ (\phi_1' - \phi_3) \ (1 + \phi_2 \ \phi_2')) +$
$(\eta_2 \ \eta_3' \ (\phi_3 - \phi_2') \ (1 + \phi_1 \ \phi_1')) +$
$(\eta_2' \ \eta_3 \ (\phi_3' - \phi_2) \ (1 + \phi_1 \ \phi_1')) +$
$((\phi_3 - \phi_3') \ (\eta_1 \ \eta_2' - \eta_1' \ \eta_2)) +$
$((\phi_2 - \phi_2') \ (\eta_3 \ \eta_1' - \eta_3' \ \eta_1)) +$
$((\phi_1 - \phi_1') \ (\eta_2 \ \eta_3' - \eta_2' \ \eta_3))$

D, the coefficient of $\sin\theta$

$(\ (1 + \phi_1 \ \phi_1') \ ((\eta_2' \ \eta_3' \ \phi_2) + (\eta_2 \ \eta_3 \ \phi_2') \ ) \ ) -$
$(\ (1 + \phi_1 \ \phi_1') \ ((\eta_2' \ \eta_3' \ \phi_3) + (\eta_2 \ \eta_3 \ \phi_3') \ ) \ ) +$
$(\ (1 + \phi_2 \ \phi_2') \ ((\eta_1' \ \eta_3' \ \phi_3) + (\eta_1 \ \eta_3 \ \phi_3') \ ) \ ) -$
$(\ (1 + \phi_2 \ \phi_2') \ ((\eta_1' \ \eta_3' \ \phi_1) + (\eta_1 \ \eta_3 \ \phi_1') \ ) \ ) +$
$(\ (1 + \phi_3 \ \phi_3') \ ((\eta_1' \ \eta_2' \ \phi_1) + (\eta_1 \ \eta_2 \ \phi_1') \ ) \ ) -$
$(\ (1 + \phi_3 \ \phi_3') \ ((\eta_1' \ \eta_2' \ \phi_2) + (\eta_1 \ \eta_2 \ \phi_2') \ ) \ )$

E, the coefficient of $\cos\theta$

$$(\, (\phi_1 - \phi_1') \; \eta_2 \; \eta_3 \; (\phi_3' - \phi_2') \,) \; +$$
$$(\, (\phi_1 - \phi_1') \; \eta_2' \; \eta_3' \; (\phi_3 - \phi_2) \,) \; +$$
$$(\, (\phi_2 - \phi_2') \; \eta_1 \; \eta_3 \; (\phi_1' - \phi_3') \,) \; +$$
$$(\, (\phi_2 - \phi_2') \; \eta_1' \; \eta_3' \; (\phi_1 - \phi_3) \,) \; +$$
$$(\, (\phi_3 - \phi_3') \; \eta_1 \; \eta_2 \; (\phi_2' - \phi_1') \,) \; +$$
$$(\, (\phi_3 - \phi_3') \; \eta_1' \; \eta_2' \; (\phi_2 - \phi_1) \,) \;$$

The number of solutions to the polar equation

The polar equation can be transformed into a fourth degree equation in $\sin\theta$ hence $\sin\theta$, has no more than 4 solutions. The solution for θ and consequently the structure are not uniquely determined by 2 views of 3 points.

A possible strategy for settling on a unique solution is to solve the polar equation for more than a single triplet of points, and then inspect the sets of solutions found for the different triplets. If the intersection of these sets contains a unique solution, it is taken as the value of θ. Through the use of a computer implementation the polar equation had been applied to numerous examples of objects in motion with the result that the correct answer can usually be found from as little as 2 views of 4 points. The next few pages illustrate how the solution is uniquely determined.

Two views of a five-point object are given. The initial coordinates of the 5 points are:
P1 = (50, 200, 25)   P2 = (20, 300, 60) P3 = (-10, 100, 15)
P4 = (70, 160, -10) P5 = (-30, 230, -40)
The transformation was R = 30 degrees, and T was (Δx = 15, Δy = 30, Δz = 20)

The solutions for the polar equation for points (P1 P2 P3) are 11.5 and 30 degrees. For (P1 P2 P4) the solutions are 2.3, 20.1 and 30 degrees. The true rotation is already recoverable since only (30) appears in both sets of solutions.

The solutions for points (P1 P2 P5) are at -13.4 and 30 degrees, confirming the previous solution.

Recovery of the Structure and Translations

Once the rotation angle θ is known, the translations and structure of the object are also computable. Recall that in perspective projection the solution is given up to scaling. The translation and structure are given here in units of $y1$ (the distance in depth of the first point) so that the computed $y2$ is in fact the ratio between $y2$ and $y1$ and similarly for the other parameters.

Computation of the translation

The translation in depth Δy can be found from any one of the points P_i by the formula:

(5)

$$\Delta y = \frac{\alpha_i \beta_1 - \alpha_1 \beta_i}{\alpha_i (\eta'_i - \eta'_1) - \beta_i (\phi'_i - \phi'_1)}$$

$$\Delta x = \alpha_1 + \phi'_1 \Delta y$$

$$\Delta z = \beta_1 + \eta'_1 \Delta y$$

Computation of the structure

The depth coordinates of P_i are given by:

(6)

$$y_i = \frac{\beta_1 + \Delta y (\eta'_1 - \eta'_i)}{\beta_i}$$

x_i and z_i can now be found as well through η_i and ϕ_i.

Application of the polar equation

Suppose that areal photographs of some terrain are taken. If the optical axis of the photographing camera is confined to a plane, (e.g. the camera is carried by an airplane in a straight and level flight or by a satellite in any quadratic orbit) the motion of the terrain relative to the camera falls under the category of Z-rotation and translations. It follows that by using the polar equation the terrain can be mapped (up to a single scaling factor) from two snapshots, *even without knowing the camera's trajectory or its position along the trajectory.* It is of interest to note that the information recovered is almost as complete as in stereoscopic mapping although neither the positions nor the orientations of the camera are known (in fact they are recovered by the computation).

The case of pure translation

An especially simple case of perspective computation arises when the object's motion involves no rotation. The case of motion in depth is no exception: like any other pure translation it is easy to compute. If no rotation is involved ($\theta = 0$), the polar equation assumes the form:

$$B + E = 0$$

This simple form can be used as a *test* for pure translation.

The usefulness of the test depends on the question of whether the equation $B + E = 0$ (which I shall call the *translation test*) can be reliably used as an indication of pure translation. The polar equation guarantees that if a set of points is actually engaged in pure translation every triplet will satisfy the translation test. However the converse is not necessarily true. Points might satisfy the test without being subject to pure translation. Application of the test to examples revealed that the test is highly reliable even for a few points. (The actual number of points depends on the accuracy of the computation, in a specific computer implementation four were usually sufficient.)

Computation of the structure

For $\theta = 0$ the coefficients α_i and β_i assume the simple form:

$$\alpha_i = \phi'_i - \phi_i \quad \beta_i = \eta'_i - \eta_i$$

Let $\delta\phi$ stand for the change in ϕ between the first and second frame, namely $\delta\phi_i = \phi'_i - \phi_i$, and let $\delta\eta_i$ denote in analogous way the change in η_i. Finally, let $\Delta\phi_i$ stand for $\phi'_i - \phi'_1$ and $\Delta\eta_i$ for $\eta'_i - \eta'_1$.

The structure in this notation is given by:

(7)

$$y_i = \frac{\delta\eta_1 \, \Delta\phi_2 - \delta\phi_1 \, \Delta\eta_2}{\delta\eta_2 \, \Delta\phi_2 - \delta\phi_2 \, \Delta\eta_2}$$

Note that the structure is given by *relative* terms only. The actual positions of the points are immaterial, the solution is based only on the distances between points and their displacements between the first and second "snapshots".

FOOTNOTES

Introduction

1 An exact definition of "idealized conditions" will not be given, since it will require discussions beyond the scope of the introduction. To illustrate by way of an example: The theory of arithmetic operations can be considered the underlying theory of the electronic calculator, although it will sometimes fail to predict the calculator's actual behavior. When such a discrepency occurs, it can be attributed to an imperfection of the calculator. In other words, the calculator is successful to the extent that it approximates the theory of arithmetic, and therefore arithmetic can be considered its underlying theory (or the theory of its "idealized operation").

2 Corroborations of the claim that apparent and "real" motion are not fundamentally different come from various sources, such as:

(1) Under appropriate conditions apparent motion cannnot be distinguished subjectively from "real" motion.
(2) Several studies (e.g. [Clatworthy & Frisby, 1973]) indicate that the same mechanism in the human visual system supports both types of visual motion.
(3) The fact that apparent motion perception has been demonstrated in many animals suggests its universal importance to natural motion perception. Also, it is probably innate, both in humans [Tauber & Koffler, 1966] and in lower animals [Rock, Tauber & Heller, 1964].
(4) Discontinuous motion can be real in the sense that it might occur in natural situations. Saccadic eye movements are one possible source of such discontinuities, eye blinks are another, and blood vessels in front of the eye receptors lamina yet another [Gregory & Gombrich, 1973; p. 73].

Whether the distinction between continuous and discrete motion is a meaningful one depends on the way motion is detected and analyzed. Consider for example the following hypothetical scheme of motion determination. Suppose that a "motion detector" for a particular element is constructed out of two individual detectors, each one tuned to detect the element at a particular location. (Such hypothetical motion detectors cannot be too low-level in nature. One reason is that it is possible to elicit apparent motion inter-ocularly and also when, due to intervening eye motion, the two stimuli fall on the same retinal location [Rock & Ebenholtz, 1962]. Julesz and Payne [1968] have shown that motion can also be established betwen the binocularly produced edges in random dots stereograms.) In such a scheme it does not matter whether the element moves continuously or in a single step from the first location to the second. One difference that does exist between these two cases is that intermediate "motion-detectors" will be activated by the continuous motion only. The main significance of the apparent motion phenomenon (in such a scheme of motion detection) is that a compelling perception of motion can be invoked without the "support" of the intermediate detectors, hardly a surprising result, considering remark (4) above. Depending on the actual mechanism for motion detection embodied in the visual system, it might be that the only distinction between real and apparent motion perception is that the latter uses only a part of the machinery used by the first. It does not follow, of course, that the two kinds of motions are indistinguishable at any level. For example: apparent motion can be invoked dichoptically, that is, when the first presentation is shown to one eye, the second to the other. No one will venture that such a motion should have, for instance, the same visual masking characteristics as a real, continuous, motion. I believe that the distinctions found so far between the two kinds of motion [Kolers, 1964; Kaufman et al., 1971] are of this nature.

3   As suggested by Kahneman and Wolman [1970], the choice of about 120 msec. presentation time has the advantage of minimizing the effects of presentation time, thus rendering the ISI the relevant timing variable.

4   At such a distance accomodation depth cues become ineffective [Power & Day, 1973].

Chapter 1

1.1   A subtraction process is similar to discrete cross-correlation with subtraction substituting for multiplication. Namely, it is a sum of the form $\Sigma |A_i - B_i|$ where A and B are the arrays to be compared. Like the cross-correlation, the subtraction process can be *global* in which case the entire arrays are compared, or *local* in which case the best match in A for a sub-region of B is sought.

1.2   The simple case in which the image does not change in shape corresponds to an object in rotary motion about the eye, like that of the moon about the earth.

1.3   See definitions in note 1.1. The local graphs were obtained by taking the sub-region of B between positions 160 and 200. The edge in picture B is at position 180.

1.4 Additional support comes from various psychological and physiological studies which indicate that form and movement are processed separately in the human visual system [Tolhurst, 1973; Frisby & Clatworthy, 1974; Sekuler & Levinson, 1977].

Chapter 2

2.1 I wish to defend the general view that the correspondence process is based on the matching of primitive basic elements, but not any particular scheme advanced in the past. I do not find the schemes based on such laws as "simplest path" and "total assimilation" ([Schiller, 1933] in [Holvand, 1935]) adequate, and I agree with Kolers' [1972] criticism of the "vector model" advanced by Brown and Voth [1937].

2.2 Michotte, as one example, included the so-called "tunnel effect" in his study of phenomenal identity. In such experiments, a moving object disappears for a part of its trajectory as if it had entered an invisible tunnel, then reappears at the other end. The question studied was under what conditions would the object retain its identity. Similarly, in some of the experiments described by Piaget [1970], objects' identity is inferred by reasoning and by long time memory comparisons, rather than by immediate perception.

2.3 The term "field" is to be understood here in its Gestalt meaning, see e.g. [Koffka, 1935].

2.4 The examples described here are from Ternus [1926]. It should be noted that the modes of correspondence he described are not always the ones actually perceived. The different modes of correspondence and some of the factors affecting them are discussed in Section 2.4.

2.5 Jones and Bruner in [Vernon 1966, p. 244] express this expectation explicitly.

2.6 In equidistant situations some observers exhibit a slight preference to the right (c.f. [Kolers, 1972; p. 65]), others to the left. The magnitude of the effect is negligible in the current context.

2.7 The distances between the line segments in the display must be sufficiently large so that the correspondence is establised between the segments as basic elements rather than between constituents thereof. See Section 2.4.2 for further comments on this point.

2.8 One problem with the simple competing motion technique is the cover property discussed in Chapter 3: The correspondence process exhibits a preference for matchings in which no element is left without a partner. There are various methods for improving the simple competing motion technique, but they will not be detailed here.

2.9 The main requirements are that the correspondence strength (Section 2.3) be monotonically increasing in the affinity function and monotonically decreasing in the competition interactions.

2.10 Another way of formulating the peripheral increase, peripheral equation, and ISI equation is to say that the affinity is also a function of position in the visual field and of the ISI. The formulation in terms of "effects" emphasizes the uniform affect of eccentricity and ISI on the affinity between pairs of tokens.

2.11 The effect of color, on which there is conflicting evidence, has not been examined. Holvand [1935] brings some evidence that color plays only a minor role in determining their correspondence, while in [Fernberger, 1934] there is some evidence to the contrary (although it might be just an intensity artifact).

2.12 Frisby and Julesz [1976] observed a similar termination correspondence in stereopsis. It is possible that terminations, and perhaps corners, are included in the set of basic elements.

2.13 All the distances in the experiment were greater than 15 minutes of visual angle, to exclude a possible interference from the short-range process mentioned in Chapter 1.

2.14 The notion of correspondence strength bears only superficial similarity to earlier notions of attraction and cohesiveness [Koffka, 1935; Brown & Voth, 1937] which Kolers [1972] correctly refutes.

2.15 Simple extensions of the competing motion configuration show that not only the weaker connection but the stronger one as well is affected by the competition.

2.16 Small identical blobs behave, as far as the affinity is concerned, similar to the dots discussed in Section 2.2. Further investigation will be required to examine the dependency of the affinty between blobs on such parameters as size and orientation.

2.17 The perceptual matches described here are in agreement with Kolers' results. Example 1 is after example 13 of Kolers [1972]; 3 and 4 are after examples 15 and 16 of Kolers [1972].

2.18 Ternus [1926] used a three-point display rather than the two-point configuration in this example.

2.19 The Gestalt researchers usually emphasized only the coherent mode. An early reference to the two-modes phenomenon (not including the ISI effect) is found in [Fernberger, 1934].

2.20 Attneave [1974] suggested that a "virtual line" drawn between the elements is responsible for the coherent mode. Such a line (which is a special case of the grouping discussed in Section 2.4.2) cannot by itself explain the *transition* between modes. Furthermore, the coherent mode holds also for elements like parallel lines between which a "virtual line" is unlikely. See also Chapter 3 for further discussion of the Ternus configuration.

2.21 It should be noted, however, that eye movements alone, with no retinal shift, are probably also sufficient to introduce supression.

Chapter 3

3.1 Another possible general strategy, which is not necessarily equivalent to maximizing the probability of a correct answer, would be to minimize the expected error.

3.2 In the case where grouping precedes the match, nearby elements will, of course, move together, but this should not concern us here. It should also be noted that although "positive interactions" do not seem necessary, they cannot be ruled out completely. In accordance with Chapter 2, it is advisable not to assume additional interactions unless their existence is strongly supported.

3.3 Most of the tangential connections in the visual cortex are rather short ranged (see e.g. [Szentagothai, 1973]). The tangential span of most cells is limited to few hundred microns, only in Lamina I and in the case of basket cells in other laminae, the tangential span is known to be larger, up to few millimeters.

3.4 The proof of this claim will not be given here. See [Ullman, 1978c] for details.

3.5 The initial candidates might be required to lie within a certain spatial neighborhood. This is one possible reason for why an element can remain without a partner. If it is too far from all the other elements, it might have no initial candidates for a match.

3.6 Such a thresholding operation will speed up the convegence, but the final solution might deviate from the ideal minimal mapping. It seems reasonable, however, to prefer a fast approximation to the minimal mapping over an accurate, but much slower, computation.

3.7 The following definition of convergence is used: for every $\varepsilon > 0$ there exist ρ and τ such that the iterative procedure will monotonically approach a saddle-point for $t < \tau$ and will remain within a distance ε from the saddle point for $t > \tau$ for any step size less than ρ. For details see [Arrow et al Chapter 10].

3.8 The relation $d = V * ISI$ is only approximately true. The presentation time of each frame must also be taken into account [Kahneman & Wolman, 1970].

3.9 For example, the correspondence pattern is unaltered when the dot-pairs in [Kolers, 1972, arrays 22,23] are replaced by short lines segments. It is altered, however, when background dots that disrupt the grouping are introduced. It seems therefore that the match is sometimes established in these examples between the group tokens rather than between the individual dots. A possibility related to the non-crossing rule is that the filling-in process (Chapter 5) is affected by the crossing paths.

3.10 A similar flow detection capacity exists in static patterns. However, it is probably based on different principles [Stevens, 1978].

3.11 If the rotation is sufficiently small it will, of course, be detected as well. Note also that the flow detection lemma will not be applicable to the minimal mapping scheme when the displacements are too large, since it will no longer be a local cover.

3.12 In perspective the angular velocity $\omega = v/r$ is measured. If no depth information is used, r can be assumed to be the same for all points. It follows that (23) could be expressed in terms of ω instead of v. It should also be noted that the assumptions used in deriving $p(v)$ are not crucial, they are used mainly to obtain an estimate on the shape of $p(v)$.

3.13 When manipulating v by changing the ISI between frames, care must be taken with regard to the effect of the presentation time. Below about 120 msec. an increase in the presentation time has similar effects to an increase in the ISI, and therefore v_i is not given simply by d_i/ISI.

3.14 It is noteworthy that the minimal mapping was developed on the basis of two-frame presentations, with a relatively small number of tokens, and long presentation times. The extension presented in Section 3.8 is a "minimal extension" of the two-frame situation, in the sense that no additional interactions are assumed. An example of a possible additional interaction is a "colinear reinforcement" between links, which would reinforce (locally) linear paths. Another possible modification is to relax the cover requirement towards the periphery of the visual field, where elements are more likely to appear and disappear.

3.15 A term coined by A. Witkin of M.I.T.

Chapter 4

4.1 As the reference list to this point is rather extensive, it has been collected here separately.
[Miles, 1931; Gibson, 1950; Wallach & O'Connell, 1953; Wallach, O'Connell & Neisser, 1953; Gibson & Gibson, 1957, Gibson, 1957; von Fieandt & Gibson, 1959; Gibson, Gibson, Smith & Flock, 1959; Green, 1961; Braunstein, 1962; Johansson, 1964; Johansson & Jansson, 1968; 1973; Hay, 1966; Borjesson & von Hofsten, 1972; 1973; Johansson, 1973; 1974; 1975; Eriksson, 1974; Badler, 1975;].

4.2 The conveyor belt display serves a second purpose. Later in the section *implicit assumptions* are introduced. The demonstration shows that no "constant velocity" implicit assumption (c.f. [von Hofsten, 1974]) is used to recover the conveyor belt's configuration.

4.3 Gibson *et al.* noted that when two moving planes are presented simultaneously, the faster plane is *not* perceived invariably as closer than the slower one.

4.4 Frequency might not be the only relevant consideration. For instance, a "zooming in" stimulus may be interpreted as either expansion or as approaching motion. It might be *safer* to always interpret it as an approaching threat.

4.5 The concepts of constraints and assumptions can often be used in equivalent ways. The interpretation process might be based on the hypothesis that proposition P holds, or it might equivalently be constrained to produce solutions that satisfy P. The term "constraint" is sometimes preferred to characterize the way the constraints are used. Rather than a hypothesis that might be suggested, weighed, and reconsidered, a constraint suggests the use of a filter that makes accessible, in a uniform unchanging way, only some of the possible interpretations.

4.6 Chomsky [1965] drew a distiction between the underlying competence and the actual performance. See also [Marr, 1977a], and footnote 1 in the introduction on the notion of an "underlying theory".

4.7 The parallel-search algorithm was devised as a part of a study in the use of parallel computers in the processing of visual information at the Institute for Advanced Computation, at Sunnyvale, California.

4.8 The main requirement from an implicit assumption is that it holds true most of the time. If an assertion is almost always false, a useful implicit assumption can still be obtained from its negation. The worst criterion is thus one which performs at about chance level. The rotation motion parallax cue which is correct slightly less than 50% of the time cannot be, therefore, of much use.

4.9 See Appendix 2 in [Ullman 1977a] for details of "undoing" the rotation. It should be noted that for the described scheme the relative depths of A and B (Figure 4.8) which are widely separated is required. This makes the scheme more prone to errors than the other parametrs of motion.

Chapter 5

5.1   Finer experiments will be required to determine whether the two interpretations are averaged in some way when the difference between them is small.

5.2   The fact that the S.f.M scheme dominates perception "under favorable conditions" raises the interesting issue of a "strength" of a perception, that can serve as a confidence-measure associated with the percept in question. Such a confidence measure seems to be applicable to a variety of visual percepts, but it will not be examined in the current work.

5.3   One such effect is the already mentioned tendency to normalize the stimuli of maximal extension to the frontal plane. A second is a possible memory effect. Under ambiguous conditions the direction of rotation might be influenced by its immediate history.

REFERENCES

Ames, A. 1951. Visual perception and the rotating trapezoid window. *Psychological Monographs, Vol. 65 (7)*, Whole No. 324.

Anstis, S. M. 1970. Phi movement as a subtraction process. *Vision Research 10*, 1411-1430.

Anstis, S. M. and Rogers, B. J. 1975. Illusory reversal of visual depth and movement during changes of contrast. *Vision Research, 15*, 957-961.

Arnheim, R. 1974. Art and visual perception Berkely and Los Angeles: University of California Press.

Arrow, K. J., Hurwicz, L., and Uzawa, H. 1958. Studies in Linear and Nonlinear Programming Stanford: Stanford University Press.

Attneave, F. and Frost, R. 1969. The determination of perceived tridimensional orientation by minimum criteria. *Perception and Psychophysics, (6B)*, 391-396.

Attneave, F. and Block, G. 1973. Apparent motion in tridimensional space. *Perception and Psychophysics, Vol. 13, 2*, 301-307.

Attneave, F. 1972. Representation of physical space. In: A. W. Melton and E. Martin (Ed.) Coding Processes in Human Memory Washington: Winston and Sons.

Attneave, F. 1974. Apparent movement and the what-where connection. *Psychologia, 17*, 108-120.

Badler, N. I. 1975. Temporal scene analysis: Conceptual descriptions of object movements. *Technical Report 80*, Department of Computer Science, Univ. of Toronto.

Bell, H. H. and Lappin, J. S. 1973. Sufficient conditions for the discrimination of motion. *Perception and Psychophysics Vol. 14, 1*, 45-50.

Borjesson, Erik and von Hofsten, Claes. 1972. Spatial determinants of depth perception in two-dot motion patterns. *Perception and Psychophysics Vol. 11, 4* 263-268.

Borjesson, Erik and von Hofsten, Claes. 1973. Visual perception of motion in depth: Application of a vector model to three dot motion patterns. *Perception and Psychophysics Vol. 13, 2,* 169-179.

Bower, T. G. R. 1966. The visual world of the infants. *Scientific American, 225,* 80-92.

Bower, T. G. R. 1966. Slant perception and shape constancy in infants. *Science, 151,* 832-834.

Bower, T. G. R. 1971. Slant perception and shape constancy in infants. *Scientific American, 225,* 30-38.

Bower, T. G. R. 1974. Development in Infancy. San Francisco: W. H. Freeman.

Braddick, O. 1974. A short-range process in apparent motion. *Vision Research, 14,* 519-527.

Braunstein, M. L. 1962. Depth perception in rotation dot patterns: effects of numerosity and perspective. *Journal of Experimental Psychology, Vol. 64, 4,* 415-420.

Brown, J. F. and Voth, A. C. 1937. The path of seen movement as a function of the vector field. *American Journal of Psychology, Vol. 49,* 543-563.

Chomsky, N. 1965. Aspects of the Theory of Syntax. Cambridge, Mass.: The M.I.T. Press.

Clatworthy. J. L. and Frisby, J. P. 1973. Real and apparent movement: evidence for a unitary mechanism. *Perception, 2(2)* 161-164.

Cohen, B. L. and Salapatek, P. 1975. Infant Perception From Sensation to Cognition. New York, San Francisco, London: Academic Press.

Corbin, H. H. 1942. The perception of grouping and apparent motion in visual space. *Archives of Psych. Whole No. 273.*

Cornsweet, T. 1970. Visual Perception. New York: Academic Press.

Cross, J. and Cross, J. 1969. The misperception of rotary motion. *Perception and Psychophysics, Vol. 5. (2),* 94-96.

References   218

Davson, H. 1969. The Eye. New York: Academic press.

Day, R. H. and McKenzie, B. E. 1973. Perceptual shape constancy in early infancy. *Perception, 2,* 315-320.

Ditchburn, R. W. 1973. Eye Movements and Visual Perception. Oxford: Clarendon Press.

Eden, M. 1962. A three-dimensional optical illusion. *Quarterly Progress Report No. 64* M.I.T R.L.E. 267-274.

Ellis, W. D. 1967. A Source book of Gestalt Psychology   New York: Humanities Press.

Epstein, w. Jansson, G. and Johansson, G. 1968. Perceived angle of oscillatory motion. *Perception and Psychophysics Vol. 3, 1A,* 12-16.

Eriksson, E. S. 1974. A theory of veridical space perception. *Scandinavian Journal of Psychology, 15,* 225-235.

Fernberger, S. W. 1934. New phenomena of apparent visual movement. *American Journal of Psychology, 46,* 309-314.

Feynman, R. 1965. The Character of Physical Law Cambridge, Mass.: The M.I.T. Press.

Fieandt, von Kai and Gibson, J. J. 1959. The sensitivity of the eye to two kinds of continuous transformations of a shadow-pattern. *Journal of Experimental Psychology, 57,* 344-347.

Fremlin, D. 1977. Personal Communication.

Frisby, J. P. 1972. The effect of stimulus orientation on the Phi phenomenon. *Vision Research, 12,* 1145-1166.

Frisby, J. P. and Clatworthy, J. L. 1974. Evidence for separate movement and form channels in the human visual system. *Perception, Vol. 3,* 87-96.

Frisby, J. P. and Julesz, B. 1976. The effect of length difference between corresponding lines on stereopsis from single and multi-line stimuli. *Vision Research, 16,* 83-87.

Garfinkel, R. S. and Nemhauser, G. L. 1972. Integer Programming. New York: Wiley & Sons.

Gibson, E. J., Gibson, J. J., Smith, O. W. and Flock, H. 1959. Motion parallax as a determinant of perceived depth. *Journal of Experimental Psychology, Vol. 8, 1,* 40-51.

Gibson, E. J. 1969. Principles of Perceptual Learning and Development. New York: Appleton-Century-Crofts.

Gibson, J. J. 1950. The perception of the visual world Boston: Houghton Mifflin and Co.

Gibson, J. J. 1957. Optical motions and transformations as stimuli for visual perception. *Psychological review, Vol. 64* (5), 288-295.

Gibson, J. J. and Gibson, E. J. 1957. Continuous perspective transformations and the perception of rigid motion. *Journal of Experimental Psychology, Vol. 54, 2,* 129-138.

Gibson, J. J. 1959. Perception as a function of stimulation. In: S Kotch (Ed.) Psychology A Study of a Science New York: McGraw-Hill.

Gibson, J. J. 1965. Research on the visual perception of motion and change. In: Spigel, I. [1965] 125-146.

Gibson, J. J. 1966. The senses considered as a perceptual system Boston: Houghton Mifflin.

Gibson, J. J. 1968. What gives rise to the perception of motion? *Psychological Review, Vol. 75, 4,* 335-346.

Graham, C. H. 1963. On some aspects of real and apparent visual movement. *Journal of the Optical Society of America Vol. 53 9,* 1019-1025.

Graham, C. H. (ed.) 1965. Vision and Visual perception New York: Wiley.

Green, B. F. 1961. Figure coherence in the kinetic depth effect. *Journal of Experimental Psychology, Vol. 62, 3,* 272-282.

Gregory, R. L. 1970 The Intelligent Eye. N.Y., St. Louis, San Francisco:

McGraw-Hill.

Gregory, R. L. and Gombrich, E. H. (ed.) 1973. **Illusions in Nature and Art** Duckworth.

Hay, C. J. 1966. Optical motions and space perception - an extention of Gibson's analysis. *Psychological Review, 73,* 550-565.

Helmholtz, H. L. F. von. 1910. **Treatise on physiological optics.** Translated by J. P. Southall, 1925, N.Y. Dover Publications.

Hershberger, W. A. 1967. Comment on apparent reversal (oscillation) of rotary motion in depth. *Psychological Review, 74* 235-238.

Hershberger, W. A. & Urban, D. 1970. Depth perception from motion parallax in one dimensional polar projection: projection versus viewing distance. *Journal of Experimental Psychology, 86,* 133-136.

Hershberger, W. A. & Urban, D. 1970. Three motion parallax cues in one-dimensional polar projection of rotation in depth. *Journal of Experimental Psychology, 86,* 380-383.

Hershberger, W. A. & Starzec, J. J. 1974. Motion parallax cues in one dimensional polar and parallel projections: Differential velocity and acceleration/displacement change. *Journal of Experimental Psychology, 103 (4),* 717-723.

von Hofsten, C. 1974. Proximal velocity change as a determinant of space perception. *Perception and Psychophysics, Vol. 15, 3,* 488-494.

Holvand, C. I. H. 1935. Apparent movement. *Psychological Bulletin., 32,* 755-778.

Jansson, G. and Johansson, G. 1973. Visual perception of bending motion. *Perception, Vol. 2,* 321-326.

Johansson, G. 1964. Perception of motion and changing form. *Scandinavian Journal of Psychology, 5,* 181-208.

Johansson, G. and Jansson, G. 1968. Perceived rotary motion from changes in a straight line. *Perception and Psychophysics, Vol. 4, 3,* 165-170.

Johansson. G. 1973. Visual perception of biological motion and a model for its analysis. *Perception and Psychophysics, Vol. 14, 2,* 201-211.

Johansson, G. 1974. Visual perception of rotary motion as transformation of conic sections -- a contribution to the theory of visual space perception. *Psychologia, 17,* 226-237.

Johansson, G. 1975. Visual Motion Perception. *Scientific American, Vol. 232, No. 6,* 76-88.

Jones, E. E. and Bruner, J. S. 1954. Expectancy in apparent visual movement. *British Journal of Psychology, 45,* 157-165.

Julesz, B. and Payne, R. A. 1968. Differences between monocular and binocular stroboscopic movement perception. *Vision Research, 8,* 433-444.

Julesz, B. 1971. Foundation of Cyclopean Perception. Chicago: The University of Chicago Press.

Kabrisky. M. 1966. A Proposed Model for Visual Information Processing in the Human Brain Urbana an London: The University of Illinois Press.

Kahneman, D. and Wolman, R. 1970. Stroboscopic motion: effects of duration and interval. *Perception and Psychophisics, Vol. 8, 3,* 161-164.

Kaufman, L. Cyrulnik, I., Kaplowitz, J., Melnick, G. and Stoff, D. 1971. The complementarity of apparent and real motion. *Psychologische Forschung, 34,* 343-348.

Koffka, K. 1935. Principles of Gestalt Psychology (280-306) New York: Harcourt, Brace and World.

Kolers, P. A. 1964. The illusion of movement. *Scientific American, 211 (4),* 98-106.

Kolers. P. A. 1966. An illusion that dissociates motion, object and meaning. *Quarterly Progress Report No. 82,* M.I.T R.L.E. 221-223.

Kolers, P. A. 1968. Some psychological aspects of Pattern Recognition. In: Kolers, P. A. and Eden, M. (ed.) 1968. Recognizing Patterns. Cambridge and London: The M.I.T Press.

Kolers, P. A. 1972. Aspects of Motion Perception New York: Pergamon Press.

Korte, A. 1915. Kinematoskopische Untersuchungen. *Zeitschrift fur Psychologie, 72,* 193-296.

Kuhn, H. W. and Tucker, A. W. 1951. Nonlinear Programming. In J. Neyman (ed.) *Proceedings of the Second Berkeley Symposium on Mathematical Statistics and Probability* Berkeley and Los Angeles: University of California Press, 481-492.

Leese, J. A., Novak, C. S. and Taylor, V. R. 1970. The determination of cloud pattern motion from geosynchronous satellite image data. *Pattern Recognition, 2,* 279-292.

Lindsay, P. H. and Norman, D. A. 1972. Human Information Processing New York and London: Academic Press.

Mach, Ernst. 1959. The Analysis of Sensations New York: Dover Publications.

Mackay, D. M. 1961. The effects of non-redundant stimulation. *Nature (London,) 192,* 739-740.

Mackay, D. N. 1970. Elevation of visual threshold by displacement of retinal image. *Nature, 225,* 90-92.

Marmolin, H. 1973. Visually perceived motion in depth resulting from proximal changes. *Perception and Psychophysics, Vol. 14, 1,* I: 133-142 II: 142-148.

Marr, D. 1974. A note on the computation of binocular disparity in a symbolic, low-level visual processor. *M.I.T. A.I. Memo, No. 326.*

Marr, D. 1976. Early Processing of visual information. *Philosophical Transactions of the Royal Society of London, Vol. 275,* 942, 483-534.

Marr, D. 1977a. Artificial Intelligence -- A personal view. *Artificial Intelligence, 9,* 37-48.

Marr, D. 1977b. Representing visual information. *M.I.T. A.I. Memo, No. 415.*

Marr, D. and Poggio, T. 1976. Cooperative computation of stereo disparity.

Science, 194, No. 4262, 283-287.

Marr, D. and Poggio, T. 1977. From understanding computation to understanding neural circuitry. *Neuroscience Research Program Bulletin, 15(3),* 470-488.

Michotte, A. 1963. The Perception of Causality. New York: Basic books Inc. (original edition in 1946, translated by T. R. Miles).

Miles, W. R. 1931. Movement interpretations of the silhouette of a revolving fan. *American Journal of Psychology, 43,* 392-505.

Navon, D. 1976. Irrelevance of figural identity for resolving ambiguities in apparent motion. *Journal of Experimental Psychology, Human Perception and Performance, 2(1),* 130-138.

Neff, Walter S. 1936. A critical investigation of the visual apprehension of movement. *American Journal of Psychology Vol. XLVIII,* 1-42.

Olson, R. K. 1974. Slant judgements from static and rotating trapezoids correspond to rules of perspective geometry. *Perception and Psychophysics, 15(3),* 509-516.

Orlansky, J. 1940. The effect of similarity and difference in form on apparent visual movement. *Archives of Psychology, 246*

Ortega, J. M. and Rheinboldt, W. C. 1970. Iterative Solution of Nonlinear Equations. New York: Academic Press.

Pantle, A. J. 1973. Stroboscopic movement based upon global information in succesively presented visual patterns. *Journal of the Optical Society of America,* 1280.

Pantle, A. J. and Picciano, L. 1976. A multistable display: Evidence for two separate motion systems in human vision. *Science, Vol. 193,* Aug. 6, 500-502.

Piaget, J. 1954. The construction of reality in the child New York: Basic Books.

Piaget, Jean. 1970. The Childs Conception of Motion and Speed Translated from French by G. E. T. Holloway and M. J. Mackenzie. New York: Basic Books.

Potter, J. 1974. The Extraction and utilization of motion in scene description. *Ph.D Thesis*, University of Wisconsin.

Power, R. P. and Day, R. H. 1973. Constancy and illusion of apparent direction of rotary motion in depth: Tests of a theory. *Perception and Psychophysics Vol. 13, 2*, 217-223.

Price K. 1975. A Comparison of human and computer vision. *ACM SIGART Newsletter 50* 5-10.

Ramachandran, V. S., Madhusudhan, V. R. and Vidyasagar, T. R. 1973. Apparent movement with subjective contours. *Vision Research, Vol. 13*, 1399-1401.

Ratliff, F. 1972. Contour and Contrast. *Scientific American, 266, (6),* 90-101.

Rock, I. and Ebenholtz, S. 1962. Stroboscopic movement based on change of phenomenal rather than retinal location. *American Journal of Psychology, 72,* 221-229.

Rock, I., Tauber, E. S. and Heller, D. P. 1964. Perception of stroboscopic movement: Evidence for its innate basis. *Science, 147,* 1050-1052.

Sekuler, R. and Levinson, E. 1977. The perception of moving targets. *Scientific American, 236, (1),* 60-73.

Shepard, R. N. and Judd, S. A. 1976. Perceptual illusion of rotation of three-dimensional objects. *Science, Vol. 191,* 952-954.

Smith, E. A. and Phillips, D. R. 1972. Automated cloud tracking using precisely aligned digital ATS pictures. *IEEE Trans. Computers, 21,* 715-729.

Sigman, E. and Rock, I. 1974. Stroboscopic movement based on perceptual intelligence. *Perception, Vol. 3,* 9-28.

Sperling, G. 1976. Movement perception in computer-driven visual displays. *Behavior research method and instrumentation, 8,* 144-151.

Spigel, I. (ed.) 1965. Readings in the Study of Visually Perceived Motion New York: Harper and Row.

Stevens, K. A. 1978. Computation of locally parallel structure. *Biological Cybernetics, 29,* 19-28

Szentagothai, J. 1973. Synaptology of the visual cortex. in: Jung, R. (ed.) 1973. Handbook of Sensory Physiology. *Vol. VII/3B.* Berlin Heidelberg New york: Springer-Verlag.

Tauber, E. S. and Koffler, S. 1966. Optomotor response in human infants to apparent motion: Evidence of innateness. *Science, 152,* 382-382.

Ternus, J. 1926. Experimentelle Untersuchung uber phanomenale Identitat. *Psychologische Forschung, 7,* 81-136. Translated in [Ellis 1967].

Toch, H. H. and Ittelson, W. H. 1956. The role of past experience in apparent motion: A revaluation. *British Journal of Psychology, 47,* 195-207.

Tolhurst, D. J. 1973. Separate channels for the analysis of the shape and movement of a moving visual stimulus. *Jouranl of Physiology, 231,* 385-402.

Traub, J. F. 1964. **Iterative Methods for the Solution of Equations.** N.J.: Prentice-Hall.

Ullman, S. 1976a. On visual detection of light sources. *Biological Cybernetics 21,* 205-212.

Ullman, S. 1976b. Filling in the gaps: on the shape of subjective cotours and a model for their generation. *Biological Cybernetics, 25,* 1-6.

Ullman, S. 1977a. The interpretation of visual motion. *M.I.T. Ph.D. Thesis, Department of Electrical Engineering and Computer Science.*

Ullman, S. 1977b. Transformability and object identity. *Perception and Psychophysics 22(4),* 414-415.

Ullmam, S. 1978a. Two dimensionality of the correspondence process in apparent motion. *Perception, 5* Forthcoming.

Ullman, S. 1978b. The interpretation of structure from motion. *Proceedings of the Royal Society of London,* Forthcoming.

Ullman, S. 1978c. Simple networks in the processing of visual information.

Forthcoming M.I.T. A.I. Memo.

Vernon, M. D. (ed.) 1966. Experiments in Visual Perception Penguin Books.

Vernon M. D. 1971. The Psychology of Perception. Pinguin Books.

Volkman, C. F. 1962. Vision during voluntary saccadic eye movements. *Journal of the Optical Society of America, Vol. 52, 5,* 571-578.

Wallach, H. and O'Connell, D. N. 1953. The Kinetic depth effect. *Journal of Experimental Psychology, 45, 4,* 205-217.

Wallach, H., O'Connell, D. N., and Neisser, U. 1953. The memory effect of visual perception of 3-d form. *Journal of Experimental Psychology, 45,* 360-368.

Wallach, H., Weisz, A. and Adams, P. A. 1956. Circles and derived figures in rotation. *American Journal of Psychology, 69* 48-59.

Wallach, H. 1959. The perception of motion. *Scientific American, 201,* 56-60.

Warren, H. W. 1977. Visual information for object identity in apparent motion. *Perception & Psychophysics, 21,* 264-268.

Weir, S. 1965. The perception of motion: actions, motives and feelings. *University of Edinburgh A.I report No. 13.*

Wertheimer, M. 1912. Experimentelle studien uber das sehen von bewegung. *Zeitschrift fur Psychologie, 61,* 161-265.

White, B. W. and Mueser G. E. 1960. Accuracy in reconstructing the arrangement of elements generating kinetic depth displays. *Journal of Experimental Psychology, Vol. 60, 1,* 1-11.

Wolferts, K. 1974. Special problems in interactive image processing for traffic analysis. *Second International Joint Conference on Pattern Recognition,* 1-2.

Zegers, R. T. 1964. The reversal illusion of the Ames trapezoid. *Transactions of the N.Y. Academy of Science, 26,* 377-400.

INDEX